SATURDAY'S CHILDREN

SATURDAY'S CHILDREN

A COMEDY
IN THREE ACTS

BY
MAXWELL ANDERSON

LONGMANS, GREEN AND CO.
55 FIFTH AVENUE, NEW YORK
39 PATERNOSTER ROW, LONDON, E.C.4
TORONTO, BOMBAY, CALCUTTA, AND MADRAS
1927

FIRST EDITION

SATURDAY'S CHILDREN

CAST OF CHARACTERS

WILLY SANDS

FLORRIE SANDS

MRS. HALEVY

BOBBY

MR. HALEVY

RIMS O'NEIL

MRS. GORLIK

Act I

The Halevy's Dining Room—June

Act II

The O'Neil's Kitchen-Dining Room—November

Act III

A Bedroom in Mrs. Gorlik's Boarding House
in East 35th Street—Three weeks later

SATURDAY'S CHILDREN

ACT ONE

The dining room of the HALEVY'S *apartment.
Large curtained window with window-seat right,
beside which is large wing chair with standard
lamp downstage of it. Upstage right is a large
1910 model Grand Rapids Buffet. Center stage
is the dining room table with four chairs around
it, and above that a small telephone table and
chair. Upstage left center is a swinging door
leading to the hall, the kitchen presumably being
right and the front door left.*

WILLY SANDS *is seated in the arm-chair, left,
reading the advertising sheet of the " Morning
World." His wife,* FLORRIE, *is seated below the
table, center, taking down the ads. as he dictates
them.* MRS. HALEVY *is at the end of the table.*

WILLY

[*Reading*] Cigar and stationery, poolroom, receipts $350 weekly, rent $80 — good lease, large
corner, good chance to build up —

FLORRIE

Wait a minute! Read slower!

3

WILLY

Oh, all right. — Cigar — stationery, poolroom, receipts $350 — rent $80 —

FLORRIE

And so with the young husband saving on his lunch like a dear and his little wife eking out the eggs and butter we just barely get through — and oh, we adore it, don't we, Willy?

WILLY

[*Reading*] — good lease, large corner, good chance to build up large newspaper route, sacrifice, terms, going South. Federal Business Exchange, 1133 Broadway.

FLORRIE

[*Taking it down*] Well, you might answer your only love and darling pride instead of going on in that cold-blooded way, dearest, — [*To* Mrs. Halevy] and little Willy is really growing more adorable every day — I just grudge every hour away from him, and so does Willy, only he thinks it's unmanly for a father to talk about his child — you know, the way most men run on — don't you, dear?

WILLY

[*Reading*] Garage, Central Park West, 160 cars at $40 direct from owner.   230 Grand Street —

FLORRIE

[*Writing*] 230 Grand Street! — Darling, please, my arm's paralyzed —

WILLY

[*Interrupting her*] And say, get this — We collect quickly, bad bills, notes, checks, partnership frauds, stocks, schemes, business transactions confidentially investigated, investors protected, civil, criminal, commercial difficulties handled by clever experienced detectives, free advice, open evenings, — I'm going to sick that gang on a certain party tomorrow —

FLORRIE

On me, I suppose —

WILLY

I said, on a certain party, and she knows who I mean. I'm going to find out the truth about the strange dark man who carries ice into the basement and converses with my wife by way of the dumb waiter. It's been going on for over a year now and our child's three months old — draw your own conclusions —

FLORRIE

Willy! You obscene beast — just for that I do think Tony is the handsomest thing —

WILLY

Well, all I can say is I wish he was married off and salted away so I could go to work with an easy mind —

FLORRIE

Married! Darling, he has seven children —

WILLY

And still handsome? What a man!

MRS. HALEVY

[*Vaguely*] Who is it, dear?

FLORRIE

Oh, just the ice-man. Willy's always teasing me about him. I'm going to run away with him sometime but we've had to put it off because he hasn't any money. He has only the ice business, you know. So I'm living on with Willy and the baby for the present.

MRS. HALEVY

Oh, Florrie, I don't know whether you ought to joke about such things —

FLORRIE

Now, mother —

WILLY

It's no joke, you know. It's Florrie's romance. Everybody has to have his romance, and if your husband's a real estate agent you fall in love with the ice-man, and if your husband's an ice-man you probably run away with a real estate agent. I know how to handle her, though. I stay so damn poor she never has enough pocket money to run away with anybody.

FLORRIE

[*Laying down her pencil and addressing* MRS. HALEVY] Isn't he the most vicious! — Will you take that back?

WILLY

Nope.

FLORRIE

[*Baby talk*] Will you take it back?

WILLY

Nope.

FLORRIE

[*Her hands in his hair*] Will you take it back?

WILLY

Nope. Hey. Hey. Yep! Yep! Sure!

FLORRIE

You take it all back?

WILLY

Sure! Say, leave me my hair — what there is of it.

FLORRIE

And does he love his Florrie?

WILLY

Sure, I do.   I never said I didn't.

FLORRIE

And does his Florrie love him?

WILLY

Gosh, I hope so.   If she does, she'll quit that.
Quit it, you hear?

FLORRIE

[*Loosening her hold*] And is it a good little secretary?

WILLY

Sure thing.

FLORRIE

The best in the world?

WILLY

Best in the world.

FLORRIE

Because it's very vain of its stenography, you see,
and it thinks a perfectly good little secretary is
being perfectly thrown away being wife and
mother for such a horrid beast!   It does think
so.

WILLY

Don't I know it?

FLORRIE

Don't you know what?

WILLY

Don't I know it thinks so?

FLORRIE

[*With a ferocious yank*] And doesn't Willy think so?

WILLY

[*Climaxing with yell*] Sure I do. She's a love and a darling and hellcat and she can take two hundred to the minute and there ain't nobody like her! Now leggo.

FLORRIE

Will he give his secretary a kiss? — Just like he used to when she really was his secretary and there weren't any babies and ice-men?

WILLY

Come on, get it over with. [*He lets her kiss him.*]

FLORRIE

And will he take her over to the band concert, just the way he used to?

WILLY

Don't you think we'd better be getting home to that kid?

FLORRIE

Isn't that devotion? He knows perfectly well his angel child won't wake up till morning and the maid would take care of him if he did! Besides, I want to see Bobby, and she hasn't come home yet, stupid. Kiss me. [*She kisses him.*]

MRS. HALEVY

I don't know why Bobby isn't here. She's never as late as this. She must have had dinner downtown.

WILLY

Probably had dinner with her boss. Probably planning to marry her boss.

FLORRIE

She certainly could if she wanted to.

WILLY

If she's a sister of yours she could.

FLORRIE

Now, Willy, explain that quick!

WILLY

Me? Oh, I just meant — I just meant any relative of yours could do anything.

FLORRIE

Not good enough, darling.   Try again.

WILLY

Well, you see, it's your fatal beauty that does it.
They all fall for you.   Realtors, icemen, princes
of Wales and Sweden, bosses — bosses especially.
I used to be a boss of one of you and look at me
now.

FLORRIE

Mother dear, did father ever talk that way?

MRS. HALEVY

No, I don't think he did, Florrie.   When we
were young, nothing was the way it is now.   But
he's beginning to do it the last few years.   He
never even used to swear until you girls grew up
— and then, he sort of learned it from you, I
guess.

WILLY

I bet he had to.   You keep a couple of girls in the
house swearing blue rings around you from morning to night and it corrupts any man's morals.
I'm getting so I swear myself.

FLORRIE

Well, I must say Bobby never did it much.
She was the sweet little thing —

MRS. HALEVY

She's been making up for it since you left. I guess it's working in an office with all those men. I used to think it was terrible but she doesn't mean anything by it.

WILLY

[*In the paper*] Well, when Florrie says damn — she means damn. You ought to hear her some morning when she breaks a tray of nursing bottles in the sink and spills the kid's formula over the ice-chest. Gee, you'd think she was a vice president.

FLORRIE

Well, that was only once, Willy.

WILLY

Once was enough. I learned a lot of new words that morning.

FLORRIE

You can read your paper now, dear.

WILLY

[*Who has been talking into his newspaper throughout this scene, and has not once changed his position*] Uh-huh.

FLORRIE

[*Sitting above table center*] Are you quite sure Bobby was coming home, mother?

MRS. HALEVY

Oh, she'd have telephoned.

FLORRIE

You know, mother, somebody ought to keep an eye on Bobby. It's so easy for a girl to drift into an affair — at that age.

MRS. HALEVY

[*Startled*] Bobby? Why, Florrie! —

FLORRIE

Yes, really, I mean it.

MRS. HALEVY

Bobby's a good girl, Florrie.

FLORRIE

Girls are awful hypocrites, mother. And the better they are the worse they can be. I'd feel a lot safer about her if she was married.

WILLY

[*Still deeper in paper*] Maybe we could kill two birds with one stone — fix something up between Bobby and our ice-man.

FLORRIE

You can read your paper, darling. You aren't so very funny.

WILLY

Yes'm.

FLORRIE

Did she turn Fred down, really?   I mean, was it final?

MRS. HALEVY

Oh yes; but you couldn't blame her for that — he was — well, he was over thirty — and bald —

FLORRIE

I know.   He wasn't a very romantic figure. Neither is old Helmcke, but he has got a lot of money.   Is he ever here any more?

MRS. HALEVY

Yes, he's here, but he's deaf, and after all he's a widower.   She's just sorry for him and doesn't want to hurt his feelings.   You know he's getting so deaf you have to write out what you want to say to him.

FLORRIE

But he's got a lot of money. — And who else is there?

MRS. HALEVY

There's the O'Neil boy; — but he's going to South America —

FLORRIE

South America —!   What for?

MRS. HALEVY

I don't know.   Just some trip he got a chance to take.   You know I did think it was getting serious, but he hasn't been here for a week or more and he's going day after to-morrow.

FLORRIE

Does Bobby mind?

MRS. HALEVY

I think she does, but her father doesn't — and she won't say a word.

FLORRIE

What a nuisance!   To have him go away!

MRS. HALEVY

He is a nice boy.

FLORRIE

Does he make any money to speak of?

MRS. HALEVY

She told me he gets just as much as she does.

FLORRIE

Oh well, they couldn't live on his $40 a week.   I wonder if Bobby sees him at the office.

MRS. HALEVY

I guess she sees him, but he's so busy about this trip —

FLORRIE

Well, I suppose that ends that —

WILLY

[*From the paper*] Yep, looks like the boy's got away. [*The telephone rings.*]

FLORRIE

Never mind, mother. I'll get it. [*At the phone.*] Yes? Yes? . . . Rims? . . . Oh, this is her sister. . . . She hasn't come home yet. . . . Oh, Mr. O'Neil? Oh, yes. . . . Just a moment. It's Rims O'Neil asking for Bobby.

MRS. HALEVY

Tell him she'll surely be home.

FLORRIE

[*Musing*] I think I'd better make it interesting for him. Was Bobby going out tonight?

MRS. HALEVY

Oh, no!

FLORRIE

Hello.   Why, Mr. O'Neil, she is going out to-night, but she'll have to be in shortly to dress, you know, and if you're nearby — yes — yes. . . . It must be a party or a dance because she couldn't get to the theatre now. . . . Oh, I know she'd like to see you but I'm afraid she

won't have much time. . . . Well, that is a
shame. . . .   Oh, you are? Oh, I see.   I'm sure
she didn't know . . . yes, I would tell her, of
course . . . yes . . . goodbye.   [*She hangs up.
A radio starts in the next room.*]

WILLY

Thin ice, my darling.

FLORRIE

Yes?

WILLY

What if they'd really had an engagement?

FLORRIE

As if I didn't find that out first!   What an opin-
ion he has of his secretary's brain!   Here she
thinks three answers ahead of him for years and
years and that's all the good it does.

WILLY

Well, Jiminetti!   You could tell the kid the truth,
couldn't you?

FLORRIE

Why, Willy, you wouldn't want me to tell the
truth to a perfect stranger? Think how it would
sound.

MRS. HALEVY

It would have been better, Florrie — It would
have been better.

FLORRIE

Now, Mother, be a sport.   I was just gambling.
One last throw — Winner take all.

WILLY

What a dame!

FLORRIE

[*Caught by the music*] Isn't the old bear pleased
with it?   It's pleased with itself! It really is!
[*Leaning over the back of the chair.*]

WILLY

You hate yourself, don't you?

FLORRIE

[*Moving towards right center, jazzily*] Don't it
just?

>   It's vain of its face,
>   It's vain of its figger,
>   It's just fat enough
>   But it mustn't get — larger.

WILLY

Rhyme it you dancing fool, *rhyme it!*

FLORRIE

Um — It never uses bad words.   [*The radio
wails.*]   Poor Dad — he's got Chinatown on that
two-syllable set of his.   Run in and help him,
Willy.

WILLY

I like it here, thanks.

FLORRIE

But supposing I wanted to talk to mother and you were in the way?

WILLY

Impossible.

FLORRIE

Oh, quite. You have finished with the dictation, Mr. Sands?

WILLY

[*Feeling the pressure*] That's all. [*He goes.*]

FLORRIE

Children, dishes and young husbands!

MRS. HALEVY

He's such a sweet boy, Florrie, you ought to be nicer to him.

FLORRIE

I'm a sweet girl and he ought to be nicer to me.

MRS. HALEVY

You really do like him, don't you, dear?

FLORRIE

I don't know. Yes, sometimes I think I do. But not often. — Mother, what do you really think about this Rims boy and Bobby? Is it kind of serious?

MRS. HALEVY

I don't know how it is with him — but Bobby's been crying her eyes out.

FLORRIE

You don't mean you've actually seen Bobby crying?

MRS. HALEVY

No, not seen her — But when she's been crying all night, I can tell in the morning.

FLORRIE

Well, if it's as bad as all that —

MRS. HALEVY

Oh, it is —

FLORRIE

Why, he'll probably keep her waiting for him for years, and then not come back at all —

MRS. HALEVY

I suppose so.

FLORRIE

Or else she'll just drift along waiting for some-body like him and the first thing we know she'll be an old maid and a public charge.

MRS. HALEVY

She's only twenty-three.

FLORRIE

Well, wasn't I married at twenty-three? It's easy to get married before you're twenty-five but afterwards try and do it. If only she wasn't such an egg!

MRS. HALEVY

[*Horrified*] Such a what?

FLORRIE

Such an egg!

MRS. HALEVY

Florrie!

FLORRIE

I know, but she's so unhatched, somehow — she doesn't know her way around the block — she never did.

MRS. HALEVY

People do wait sometimes — sometimes they wait for years — and then it comes out all right. We waited —

FLORRIE

Oh, I know, but that was different.

MRS. HALEVY

Yes, I suppose so.   It was all different then.

FLORRIE

[*A door closes outside.*]   Maybe that's her now.
[*She goes toward the hall door.*]

FLORRIE

Bobby, dear, I haven't seen you for an age!

BOBBY

[*Entering*] Well, why should you, darling? Don't
be sloppy. Ugh, I've just come from the subway!
Let me at the bath-tub before you kiss me.

FLORRIE

We've been waiting to see you.

BOBBY

How's the baby?

FLORRIE

Wonderful.

MRS. HALEVY

Have you had dinner, dear?

BOBBY

[*Taking off an orchid*] I don't know.   Yes, I
guess so.

MRS. HALEVY

You don't know?

BOBBY

Yes — I was — I was in a place where they were eating.   It must have been dinner.

FLORRIE

Fascinating company?

BOBBY

Just the boss.   Mengle.

FLORRIE

Since when does Mr. Mengle take you to dinner?

BOBBY

Ever since six o'clock and it's been a long time.

FLORRIE

And his conversation was so charming you couldn't think of food?

BOBBY

[*Vague and a little bored*] I hope he didn't lay himself out to be charming because I didn't hear a word he said.

FLORRIE

Well, dearest, when you go to dinner with a man you ought to at least listen to him.

BOBBY

I'll get him to say it over again sometime.   He won't mind.   If he does he can always fire me.

FLORRIE

Well, you needn't have worried and spoiled poor
Mengel's evening, for Rims did telephone, if
that's what you want to know.

BOBBY

Rims? Rims telephoned?

FLORRIE

I think that's the name.   Rims — Rims Mur-
phy —

MRS. HALEVY

O'Neil, dear.

FLORRIE

Oh, yes, O'Neil.

BOBBY

What did he say?

FLORRIE

He wanted to know if you'd be in this evening.

BOBBY

Oh.

FLORRIE

I said you were going to a dance or something,
but if he came right over —

BOBBY

Oh, I'm not going anywhere.

FLORRIE

Well, why tell him that? You don't want him to think you're sitting home weeping about him?

BOBBY

Why should he think I'm weeping? Did you know I wasn't going out?

MRS. HALEVY

I told her you weren't, Bobby —

BOBBY

Then I don't see what occasion there was for —

FLORRIE

Child, you'll never know; you'll never, never know. You're just that innocent.

BOBBY

Oh — well, he'll know I wasn't going anywhere — because I'll be here.

FLORRIE

Couldn't you change your mind? At any rate you can't tell him you weren't going out because I told him you were.

BOBBY

Couldn't you be mistaken, dear? I think you could. I even think you were.

FLORRIE

You would!

BOBBY

I think it's perfectly silly.

FLORRIE

You're quite hopeless, darling — I doubt if I can do anything for you, but I can tell you this.

BOBBY

Yes?

FLORRIE

If you want a man to be interested in you, let him see you going out the door with another man. And if you want a man to come running, just let him imagine you at a dance with someone else.

BOBBY

You're pretty tiresome tonight, Florrie. If I cared enough about anybody to want to keep him — I'd care too much to want to keep him that way.

FLORRIE

My God, can anybody be as young as that and live!

MRS. HALEVY

Well, Bobby is right, Florrie — Bobby is right!

FLORRIE

Mother, you never grew up a day after you were married.

MRS. HALEVY

Well — I'm glad I've stayed young then.

FLORRIE

Do you know what I want you to do?

BOBBY

It doesn't matter.   I wouldn't do it.

FLORRIE

I want you to put on your prettiest party dress. You were going to a dance, you see, and then Rims'll come in and you'll decide not to go.   It just gives you a chance to look your best.   Don't you see?

BOBBY

You must think I'm mad about this Rims.

FLORRIE

Aren't you, dear?

BOBBY

Not the least in the world.

FLORRIE

Oh, well, don't do it then.   Because if you did he might ask you to marry him or something and then you'd have to turn him down and it'd be such a bother.

BOBBY

Yes, I know. There's nothing like a proposal to spoil an evening. I've been so unfortunate that way.

MRS. HALEVY

Well, you have had two in a week, Bobby.

BOBBY

Three, mother.

FLORRIE

Was it Mengle?

BOBBY

Yes, I think that's what he was talking about a good deal of the time — whenever he wasn't talking about the music business. The music business, by the way, is very good.

MRS. HALEVY

But Mr. Mengle's married, dear.

BOBBY

Oh, this wasn't a proposal of marriage. It was just a — proposal.

MRS. HALEVY

But Bobby — you can't work for a man like that!

FLORRIE

Oh, I wouldn't say that, mother.

BOBBY

— No — you see, I think probably I got the job because he had hopes of me. Hope springs eternal in the employer's breast.

MRS. HALEVY

What did you say to him?

BOBBY

I didn't disillusion him completely. It's better for Mr. Mengle's hopes to go on springing eternal.

MRS. HALEVY

He must be a beast —

BOBBY

He's a rather friendly old beast, and very considerate, really.

FLORRIE

He didn't mean anything, mother.

MRS. HALEVY

But it's really terrible — for a young girl —

FLORRIE

Will you put on the party dress?

BOBBY

I might if I had one.

FLORRIE

The pink one!

BOBBY

[*She pauses, looking at Florrie, decides it is not worth arguing about. She reaches in her bag and pulls out a coin*] Heads or tails.

FLORRIE

Heads!

BOBBY

[*Flipping it*] You win.

FLORRIE

The pink dress.

BOBBY

Anything you say.

MRS. HALEVY

I must say she never would have done it if I'd asked her.

FLORRIE

Use just the right touch and you can get her to do anything. You see, mother, she's just a child. There's a psychologist writing for the American that says people don't really begin to think until they're nearly thirty. They walk around and talk and they seem human, but they're really practically unconscious.

MRS. HALEVY

I do wish you wouldn't read the American, dear.

FLORRIE

Well, sometimes I think it's really true. That's one reason why it's easy for a girl to get married young, and not so easy afterward. The idea is to catch your man while he's still unconscious. If he begins to think about it there really isn't any reason why he should get married at all. And so the psychologist says the only hope for a girl is to start thinking young and that's why girls have to be cleverer than men.

MRS. HALEVY

I don't know how people ever think of such things.

FLORRIE

He's paid to. I could think of nearly anything if I was paid to. [*There is a terrible crash of wood and metal in the next room.*]

MRS. HALEVY

Good Heavens! Merlin what did you do to it?

MR. HALEVY

[*Entering from left*] Nothing.

FLORRIE

But it sounded as if —

MR. HALEVY

It will sound no more, my darling. The infernal machine that wrecked our peace is forever silenced.

MRS. HALEVY

What have you *done?*

MR. HALEVY

[*Filling his pipe*] I have murdered the entire Philadelphia Symphony Orchestra, from Stokowski to the timpani player. I tried everything else on that Goddam machine and it didn't do any good, so I tried smashing it. From now on if we want any music we'll go where it is.

MRS. HALEVY

I don't know what's come over you, Merlin. You're so sudden lately.

MR. HALEVY

Yeah! Toward the end of his life the human male, having learned there is nothing to be gained by gentleness and compromise, begins to assert himself. You didn't want me to build a radio and I built it anyway. After I got it built I didn't like it so I smashed it. If you tell me to get another one I won't. If you tell me not to get another one I will.   [WILLY *enters from left with a newspaper in his hand.*]

FLORRIE

It's best not to tell him anything, mother.

MRS. HALEVY

Goodness knows I never tried to tell him anything.

FLORRIE

As for Willy it wouldn't dream of trying to tell him anything, would it?

WILLY

Darling, how would I know anything if you didn't tell me?

FLORRIE

You wouldn't.

WILLY

Not a thing.   [*The telephone rings.*]

FLORRIE

[*Answering it*] Hello!   No.   Oh, hello!   Oh, yes.   Mr. O'Neil?   Oh, I see.   Yes, she is . . . I think she's taking a bath — [BOBBY *pokes her head in at door up left*] what? . . .

BOBBY

Who is it?

FLORRIE

[*Into the mouthpiece*] Just a moment. [*She covers the mouthpiece*] It's this Rims fellow. The one you aren't mad about.

BOBBY

Let me talk to him.

FLORRIE

No, dear. You're supposed to be taking a bath. [*Into the phone*] Hello, — why, she is in the tub and I hate to — yes — Why she seemed rather particular about this engagement, but I'm sure she'll wait if you put it that way.

BOBBY

[*Standing up left fixing belt of wrapper*] You fiend — give me that phone!

FLORRIE

[*Covering the mouthpiece*] Go away, dear. [*Into the phone*] Just somebody cutting in, I guess. —

BOBBY

[*Grabbing phone*] Give me that phone. Hello, hello. . . . It's Bobby. . . . I was, but I heard the telephone, and . . . Oh, Rims, that's sweet of you, really. . . . I know you must be perfectly tied up . . . no, Rims, truly I'm not.

. . .   I haven't any engagement the least in the
world. . . .   It was just that infernal sister of
mine. . . .   I don't know, just her little joke, I
guess . . . anyway, I'll be here — yes, good-bye.
[*She hangs up.*]

MRS. HALEVY
Florrie, what did you mean —

BOBBY
After this I'll answer the telephone for myself,
thanks.

FLORRIE
Well, you've managed to ruin —

MR. HALEVY
What's the row about, girlies?

FLORRIE
Nothing whatever.

WILLY
I gather Florrie thinks Bobby's going out tonight
and Bobby thinks she isn't.

MR. HALEVY
Well, Bobby ought to know.

MRS. HALEVY
Now, what's Rims going to think?

BOBBY

I'll tell him exactly what happened.

FLORRIE

Well, he won't believe you.

BOBBY

Of course he'll believe me.

FLORRIE

You mean to say you're coming out in that pink dress and tell him you weren't going anywhere?

BOBBY

I'm not wearing my pink dress —

FLORRIE

No?   I thought I won the toss, my darling.

WILLY

Let us in on it.   What's the gag?

BOBBY

It's too silly to talk about.   I'm sure I don't know what Florrie thinks she's doing.   I'm going to dress.

FLORRIE

We're all going over to the concert.

BOBBY

You mean you're maneuvering everybody out of the house just to — ?   Well, I won't have it — Dad, you won't go?

MR. HALEVY

Not if you'd rather I didn't, Bobby, but the radio's out of commission and I did want some music.

BOBBY

Oh, very well.

MR. HALEVY

But I'd just as soon stay, honey, — almost —

BOBBY

Never mind —

FLORRIE

The pink dress!

BOBBY

Very well. [*She goes into bedroom.*]

MR. HALEVY

What's up, Florrie?

MRS. HALEVY

Are we going to the park?

FLORRIE

Yes! Put something on, mother — he's coming right over. It's her Rims, dad — her marvellous Rims O'Neil — and we're just clearing out to give them elbow room —

MR. HALEVY

Well, if she doesn't want us to go —

FLORRIE

Of course she does.   Only she thinks it looks too
deliberate, as if he'd think of that —

MR. HALEVY

I thought he'd gone to South America —

FLORRIE

Well, he is going but he hasn't gone yet. That's
the point, and the kids ought to have a chance to
say goodbye.

MR. HALEVY

Well, if that's all —

WILLY

[*Coming out of paper*] Say, Florrie, listen! —
You remember that little house on a hundred
and forty-first — the one we wanted? —

FLORRIE

Of course, it remembers —

WILLY

Well, it's for rent —

FLORRIE

No, not the very one —

WILLY

Sure thing — the one we wanted — and reasonable too —

FLORRIE

How much?

WILLY

Sixty.

FLORRIE

Why that's less than our apartment. Now, why did we sign that lease?

MR. HALEVY

Sixty a month for a whole house — ?

FLORRIE

Well, it's only two rooms and a kitchen, really —

WILLY

Sort of lost and forgotten among the apartment buildings —

FLORRIE

It's the funniest little place —

MR. HALEVY

Oh, well, if it's only two rooms.

FLORRIE

And a garden, dad, we simply adored it —

WILLY

We figured we could use part of the kitchen for a dining room, you see —

FLORRIE

Oh, well — [*To* MRS. HALEVY] Listen, mother, I think I'd better wait a minute and make my peace with the kid. Take Willy with you and I'll meet you there —

MR. HALEVY

Where we always sit?

FLORRIE

Yes, the same place.

WILLY

Come on, mother.

MR. HALEVY

You two run along. I'll catch up. I want to see her a minute myself —

WILLY

[*Going out with* MRS. HALEVY] Goodbye Bobby!

BOBBY

Goodbye Willy.

MR. HALEVY

Bobby! Dressed yet?

BOBBY

[*Entering left, still doing up the last few hooks of her dress*] Yeah! — what is it, dad?

MR. HALEVY

Anything the matter?

BOBBY

I guess not.

MR. HALEVY

I mean, is the kid happy?

BOBBY

Not very. Of course I'm happy.

MR. HALEVY

Well, be yourself, girlie. Don't let anybody run over you.

BOBBY

All right, dad.

MR. HALEVY

And, well, — don't do anything I wouldn't do —

BOBBY

Tell me something you wouldn't do.

MR. HALEVY

Not a damn thing I didn't feel like doing. So long. [*He goes out.*]

BOBBY
All right.

MR. HALEVY
[*Off stage*] Remember that.

BOBBY
[*To* FLORRIE] Aren't you going?

FLORRIE
You don't like me much, do you?

BOBBY
No.

FLORRIE
Well, I'll run along.

BOBBY
Oh, stay if you want to.

FLORRIE
I was just trying to make things easier for you, dear.   You're in love with Rims, aren't you?

BOBBY
No.

FLORRIE
Oh, well, then I'm sorry, and it was foolish.   But, gee, kiddie, you're a rave in that dress.   I wish somebody was coming you were in love with.

BOBBY

Thanks awfully.

FLORRIE

Will you make it up with me, dear? Because I really thought it was good fun —

BOBBY

Oh, why don't you go? Why didn't you go with the others?

FLORRIE

Bobby, you are in love with him.

BOBBY

I'm not in love with anybody that isn't in love with me.

FLORRIE

But he is.

BOBBY

No he isn't, if he was he'd have — well, it doesn't matter only I wish you'd go.

FLORRIE

It's all right, dear. I'll go the minute he comes. And listen — he is in love with you. I know by his voice over the phone. And if you want him, dear, don't you know you can have him?

BOBBY

[*Looking away*] He's going to Buenos Ayres to start a branch house.   It may take two years.

FLORRIE

Don't let him.

BOBBY

If he wants to go, why shouldn't he?

FLORRIE

Because you're in love with each other, and you'd be much happier if he stayed here, wouldn't you?

BOBBY

It doesn't matter.

FLORRIE

You know what will happen?   He'll fall in love with someone else.

BOBBY

Well, so will I, probably.

FLORRIE

You thought he was going to ask you to marry him, didn't you?

BOBBY

Yes.

FLORRIE

And if he'd stayed a little longer he would have, wouldn't he?

BOBBY

Yes.

FLORRIE

Then he'll ask you tonight.

BOBBY

No he won't. He's made up his mind not to.

FLORRIE

Darling, he didn't tell you that?

BOBBY

No, but I know.

FLORRIE

Oh, if I could only be in your shoes half an hour — just half an hour — wouldn't I get it out of him!

BOBBY

What would you do?

FLORRIE

I'd tease him — till he was wild.

BOBBY

Well, I won't.

FLORRIE

I guess you're just too good to live.

BOBBY

No, it isn't that.   I like him too much to cheat him into anything.

FLORRIE

Darling, if you knew just half a dozen sentences to say that would make him propose to you, would you say them?

BOBBY

No, I wouldn't.

FLORRIE

It's so easy — When he asks if you weren't really going out with somebody, tell him you were going out with Fred — has he ever seen Fred?

BOBBY

No, but you're just wasting your time, Florrie. [FLORRIE *turns to table, rises, gets pad and pencil.*]

FLORRIE

Look, dear, I'm writing it down — can you read my shorthand?

BOBBY

I could if I wanted to —

FLORRIE

You're going with Fred to a dance or a supper-club — you see? — and then Rims will come in and ask you to stay with him this evening — and you'll say yes, you'll call it off when Fred telephones — and then I'll telephone — isn't it easy?

BOBBY

It doesn't interest me.

FLORRIE

Then he'll ask you to go somewhere with him and you'll suddenly take out your hanky and begin to cry a little and say you don't want to go anywhere.

BOBBY

Me — cry — me?

FLORRIE

Yes, darling, you. You'll weep a little and he'll ask you what's the matter and try to comfort you, and —

BOBBY

I can't cry on order —

FLORRIE

Oh, yes, you can, dear.

BOBBY

Anyway, I never cry.

FLORRIE

Well, he'll ask you what's the matter, and then you'll say, " Oh, I'm so tired of — of everything, Rims — and I'm afraid I'm not very good company," — and he'll say, " Oh, yes, you are," and he'll put his arm around you — or would he?

BOBBY

How could he help it?

FLORRIE

Well, after that it gets easier all the time — you just say, " Rims dear, sometimes you're the only person in the world I can talk to — sometimes I can't bear to be with anybody else " —

BOBBY

I simply couldn't —

FLORRIE

But that's exactly what you've got to say — and then you go right on and say, " Rims, don't you ever get tired of poor me, — ever? "

BOBBY

And then he'd say " Never," of course.

FLORRIE

Of course — and you say, " You're such a darling — and it's going to be awfully hard " —

BOBBY

What is?

FLORRIE

That's exactly what he'll say — " What is? " and you'll say, " Marrying somebody else! "   Then he'll draw back and say, " You getting married? " and you'll say, " Oh, Rims, a girl has to get married sometime, you know, while she's got chances," and he'll say, " How many chances do you get in a week? " or something like that, and you'll say, " I've had two every other week for two weeks," or something, and he'll say " Now kid, you don't mean you've set to marry somebody? " and then you'll say —

BOBBY

Oh, no, I won't —

FLORRIE

Yes, you will, dear, you'll say, " Fred wants me to marry him, and he's awfully in love with me and I don't want to go on working forever," and he'll say, " Well, if you're getting married this season, why not marry me? " — and there you are —

BOBBY

No, because he wouldn't say it —

FLORRIE

Why not?

BOBBY

Because he isn't such a sap for one thing, and for another I don't think it's fair and I wouldn't do it.

FLORRIE

My darling, how do you think people get married?

BOBBY

I don't know.

FLORRIE

I'll say you don't —

BOBBY

Honestly, do you think a person of any sense would fall for a deliberate trap like that?

FLORRIE

Why, honeybunch, hundreds of thousands of them fall for it every year. [*The doorbell rings.*] There's one coming now. I'm running along, dear. And, look, I'm leaving those notes — see? —

BOBBY

You'd better take them —

FLORRIE

Shut the note-book if you feel scrupulous — you'll probably remember the system anyway —

it comes natural — Bye-bye! I'll just pass him in the door. [*She goes out.*] Oh, pardon me!

RIMS

[*Off-stage*] That's all right!

FLORRIE

[*Off*] I was just going out.

RIMS

[*Off*] Is Miss Halevy in?

FLORRIE

[*Off*] Miss Halevy? Oh yes. — Bobby!

BOBBY

Yes.

FLORRIE

[*Off*] Someone for you —

RIMS

[*Off*] O'Neil's the name —

FLORRIE

[*Off*] Mr. O'Neil —

BOBBY

Oh, Rims, come in!

FLORRIE

[*Off*] Goodbye, dear —

BOBBY

Goodbye, Florrie — [*Rims enters*] Hello, Rims.

RIMS

Hello, darling!   Say!

BOBBY

You say it!

RIMS

Flaming youth!   Bobby, you're a dream in that!
Stand still and let me gaze at you!

BOBBY

You like it?

RIMS

Do I?   Why haven't I seen you in that before?

BOBBY

I just made it.

RIMS

You made it?   Say, I wish you'd make my clothes
for me for a while.   I'd have them falling for me
from the third story windows!

BOBBY

Oh, any old clothes will do in Buenos Ayres.
They say they fall easy down there.

RIMS

Yeah?

BOBBY

They say it's the climate.

RIMS

I'll bet the climate can't raise 'em any sweeter
than you are because they don't come any sweeter
— Say, you were stepping out somewhere,
weren't you?

BOBBY

No, I wasn't.

RIMS

Sure, your sister said you had a heavy date on.

BOBBY

Well, I didn't.

RIMS

You're a poor liar, kid, if that's anything against
you —

BOBBY

But I say I didn't have a date —

RIMS

What's the dress for — just trying it on?

BOBBY

No, it was to settle a bet —

RIMS

I'll bet it was — Anyway I'm sorry for the other guy and it's sweet of you to turn down a dance for me —

BOBBY

Wait a minute. I haven't turned it down yet —

RIMS

Is he coming for you?

BOBBY

He's going to telephone.

RIMS

Aw, give him the air, sweetheart. I want to talk to you. I haven't seen you for a week.

BOBBY

All right. Only it isn't my fault you haven't seen me, you know —

RIMS

[*As he turns chair around and sits right center facing Bobby*] Gee, nobody's seen me. I haven't been able to see myself in the mirror the rate I was travelling. I've learned more about the Argentine in the last week than I ever knew about New York — principal cities, population, theatres, cabarets, rates of exchange, sheet music sales, what the girls like to dance to, how late they stay up — you ought to hear old Juan giving me a quiz —

BOBBY

So you're really going?

RIMS

It certainly looks that way — of course, the boss hasn't actually O.K.'d it yet but he seems to be sold on it —

BOBBY

Oh, so far as he's concerned it's going through.

RIMS

How do you know?

BOBBY

Well, I found out.

RIMS

Great stuff! Has he settled on me to go, do you know?

BOBBY

Oh, absolutely!

RIMS

You know I don't know a damn thing about it; old Juan's been coaching me but I'm pretty

dumb, I guess.   And there's a lot of fellows at the
office that rank me for experience — But say,
that's great, kid.

BOBBY

Of course, it's in confidence. —

RIMS

Sure thing.   How'd you find out?   Dictation?

BOBBY

He told me.

RIMS

He didn't talk it over with you?

BOBBY

I had dinner with him.

RIMS

Say, that's not so good, girlie.   That bird's a
pirate.

BOBBY

Well, I have to have dinner with somebody, don't
I?   And you haven't been giving anybody much
competition —

RIMS

It wasn't because I didn't want to, though. You
know every night I've thought maybe I could

get away and then some damn complication fixed
it so I couldn't.

BOBBY

Oh, I know.

RIMS

You know I haven't seen you since — Well —

BOBBY

Think hard.

RIMS

Gosh, it seems like a month.

BOBBY

Just a week ago tonight.

RIMS

You're right. And Mengle sprung this thing on
me the next day. You mean I haven't seen you
since that night on the bus?

BOBBY

Really, don't you remember?

RIMS

Gee, I'm a wash-out, girlie; this thing's wrecked
me. Say, I wish you were coming along.

BOBBY

Maybe Mengle'll let you have a stenographer —

RIMS

No chance, I guess.   He's doing this on a shoe-string — the way he does everything.   Anyway, I'm not the boss — Old Juan's in charge; I'm just a kind of super-cargo.   They've got to have some-body that can write English . . . well . . . it was certainly a nice Spring while it lasted.

BOBBY

The best I ever had, Rims.

RIMS

Me too.   You know Bobby, I'll never see a Fifth Avenue bus without thinking of you, never.

BOBBY

You won't see one for a while, though.

RIMS

That's true — but a postcard of Grant's Tomb or the Soldier's and Sailor's monument would do just as well —

BOBBY

I'll send you one with an X to mark the spot on it.

RIMS

Which spot, though?   The route's sprinkled with 'em.

BOBBY

Well, where you said your poem to me, for instance.

RIMS

Yeah? Well, it wasn't much of a poem if you ask me.

BOBBY

Rims, it was a lovely poem!

RIMS

I thought it was pretty good at the time — but I guess it was pretty rank — I don't think I'm going to try poetry again for a while —

BOBBY

Not till you fall in love again, I suppose.

RIMS

No, that's the kind of thing only happens once.

BOBBY

Anyway, it's the only poem anybody ever wrote for me — [*She says it musingly.*]

When Bobby comes to the office
The boss takes off his frown;
She wears a coat of powder blue
And a powder blue gown.
She sits upon her office chair —

RIMS

You always make me think it's good, the way you
can say it — [*The telephone rings*] If that's your
playmate tell him your're busy, will you?

BOBBY

Do you want to stick around, really?

RIMS

Sure I do.

BOBBY

[*At the telephone*] Hello. Oh, yes. Why, Fred,
[*She turns her back on Rims*] I'm awfully sorry,
but I can't go. No, really I can't. No, don't
come over, please. It isn't that. I'll tell you
when I see you. I'm awfully sorry. Yes. Goodbye. [*She hangs up and turns to face him, radi-
ant.*] There!

RIMS

You're a brick, Bobby.   Are you sure you didn't
want to go?

BOBBY

If I'd wanted to — I would have.   [*There is a
pause.*]

RIMS

I've been wanting to talk to you.

BOBBY

What about, Rims?

RIMS

Do you think it's a good thing — me going to South America?

BOBBY

It's an awfully good opening.

RIMS

Well, what I mean is, don't you think it's a good thing for a young fellow to see the world a little when he gets a chance — just so he can kind of make up his mind what he wants to do?

BOBBY

Surely.

RIMS

That's why I'm going, really.   Oh, I'm not sure it's any great shakes of an opening, but I never have been much of anywhere and it's a chance — well, it's a kind of adventure, don't you see?

BOBBY

Surely.

RIMS

[*At a loss*] That's why I'm going.

BOBBY

Yes.   [*A pause.*]

RIMS

And, kid —

BOBBY

Yes?

RIMS

[*Placing a hand on her arm*]   You certainly have
been wonderful to me.

BOBBY

We did have a good Spring together, didn't we?

RIMS

You were certainly marvellous.   [BOBBY *looks at
him, and then turns away.*]

BOBBY

Well, it's Summer now.

RIMS

Yep.   But that's no reason you shouldn't give me
a kiss, is it?

BOBBY

I guess not.   [*They kiss.*]   Maybe you'd better
run along, Rims.

RIMS

Why so, sweetie?   The night's young.

BOBBY

Well — [*She looks down and her eye falls on Florrie's notebook.   She looks at it fascinated. There is a pause.*]

RIMS

[*Lightly*] What you studying, Bobby?

BOBBY

Nothing.   Only — oh, I'm so tired of everything, Rims, and I'm afraid I'm not very good company.

RIMS

Oh, yes, you are.

BOBBY

Rims, dear —

RIMS

Yes.

BOBBY

[*She looks back at book*] Rims, sometimes you're the only person in the world I can talk to.   Sometimes I can't bear to be with anybody else.

RIMS

Gee, kid.

BOBBY

Rims, don't you ever get tired of poor me, ever?

RIMS

Never, I should say not.

BOBBY

You're such a darling.

RIMS

Well, I wouldn't say that.

BOBBY

But you are, [*She turns and glances at the note-book*] and it's going to be awfully hard. [*A pause.*]

RIMS

What is, sweetheart?

BOBBY

Marrying somebody else.

RIMS

You getting married? [*His hand drops from her shoulder*]

BOBBY

Oh, Rims, a girl's got to get married sometime you know, while she's got chances.

RIMS

I suppose you get chances all right.

BOBBY

Yes.

RIMS

Do they come fast?

BOBBY

I've had two — every other week, for two weeks.

RIMS

Say, look here, you don't mean you're making up
your mind to marry somebody in particular?

BOBBY

Well, Fred wants me to marry him, and he's awfully in love with me, and I don't want to go on
working forever.

RIMS

I see. Yeah, I see. I didn't know you felt that
way.

BOBBY

[*Breaking away*] Well, I don't, really. I was
just — I was just joking. You'd better go, dear.
I wouldn't marry anybody. I wouldn't marry
— anybody. Not even you.

RIMS

You wouldn't?

BOBBY

No, I wouldn't!

RIMS

Oh, yes, you will.   I mean —

BOBBY

Do you want me too?

RIMS

Sweetheart — I don't want anything else.   [*They kiss.*]

BOBBY

[*Breaking away and crying on his shoulder*] But you're — you're going to South America —

RIMS

[*Still holding her*] South America can go to the devil — !   Somebody else can go to South America!

CURTAIN

ACT TWO

The O'NEILS' *kitchen-dining room. There is
the back door right, reached by passing through
a shallow closet with props, brooms, pails, etc.
Down right facing up center is a small chair. Up
right is the stove and beside it a kitchen table.
Next to the kitchen table is the sink with a rack
of Gold Dust, Rinso, etc., above it. Left is an
arch, with French-windows leading to living
room, and front door. This has a table, a standard lamp, and an armchair visible. There are
windows up right and up left.*

BOBBY *is standing left by table clearing the dishes
away after supper.* RIMS *is off left in the living
room.*

RIMS

[*Off left*] Where the devil are my pipe cleaners?

BOBBY

I should know.

RIMS

Well, I certainly put some here and I didn't move
'em.

67

BOBBY

Oh, dear, I took all the things off that desk
because I had to set the lamp somewhere when the
folks came —

RIMS

[*Off*] I knew you took 'em.

BOBBY

Why, Rims, I didn't take them.   I moved them
because I had to.   What do you think I did with
them?

RIMS

[*Off*] I give up.

BOBBY

[*Going in to help him*] Silly.   I'll find them.

RIMS

Oh, hell, I'm all out of tobacco.   Where's my
cigarettes?

BOBBY

[*Re-entering*] Oh, here they are.   Mine were all
gone.

RIMS

Gosh, there's only one left.

BOBBY

[*She picks up her cigarette*] That's all right.   I've
got one.

RIMS

Yeah, but I had half a package here.

BOBBY

I know. I asked you to bring me some last night, but I guess you forgot it. —

RIMS

[*Lighting cigarette*] Well, I didn't really forget it, only I was running so low on cash —

BOBBY

But you got paid to-day.

RIMS

Yeah, only I did forget 'em this afternoon.

BOBBY

You see. I thought sure you'd bring some, dear.

RIMS

[*Throwing match in ash tray, and smoking contentedly*] It's all right.

BOBBY

I don't see how you could be low in cash. You don't eat it all, do you?

RIMS

What do you expect on five dollars a week?

BOBBY

You never seem to have any money.

RIMS

Well, now, the truth is, I took a couple of passes at peanuckle last week, and they ruined me.

BOBBY

But, Rims, if you do that —

RIMS

Hell, I'm not dead yet, you know.

BOBBY

We've got to stick to the budget, dear, or we'll never come out even.   I've been over everything this afternoon and it's awfully close figuring.

RIMS

We're going to be lucky if we get by.

BOBBY

[*Flashing*] I wish you wouldn't talk that way, Rims. There's no luck about it.   It's just figures. [*She gets out her account book.*]   Listen — this is the way it adds up.

RIMS

Say, kiddie, spare me the horrible details.

BOBBY

No, it's the treasurer's report — you've got to hear it or we can't co-operate.

RIMS

You know I've tried that and it doesn't do any good.

BOBBY

But you didn't stick to it, then!

RIMS

Hell, I couldn't. Every time I thought I had it all worked out some damn thing would come along and sink me for a month. I know.

BOEBY

Well, listen, anyway.

RIMS

All right.

BOBBY

Well, we get $240 a month and when there's five weeks in a month we get $300.

RIMS

Sounds like too much money — how much is it in a year?

BOBBY

Don't interrupt. Two hundred and forty a month and out of that we pay sixty for rent, about thirty-five for groceries, forty on the furniture, twenty for your allowance, ten insurance,

about six for gas and light, and about three for
ice.   And it comes to a hundred and seventy-
four.

RIMS

You must have left something out.

BOBBY

[*Still intent*] Please!   A hundred and seventy-
four from two hundred and forty leaves sixty-
six dollars —

RIMS

Then how do I happen to be broke all the time?

BOBBY

Of course, if it doesn't interest you —

RIMS

Sure it interests me, Bobby.   You know, I've got
a great idea, girlie.   How about a little game of
black jack for that sixty-six dollars?

BOBBY

Rims, you idiot!   If you don't take me seriously
I'll never — never —   You can take care of your
own dirty old money!   I can earn some for myself!

RIMS

Ah, take it easy, Bobby.   I was only fooling.

BOBBY

Will you really listen?

RIMS

Sure I will! Geez, I've been listening.

BOBBY

Oh, it isn't any use. You don't think it matters . . . but I *know* it does.

RIMS

[*Mock-serious*] Don't I know it matters? Why, kid, if you can figure out how we can save sixty-six a month—well—you're good.

BOBBY

I didn't say we could save that much. We have to use that for clothes and dentist and doctor's bills and extras—

RIMS

No, say, there's certainly something wrong here—

BOBBY

But just a minute. I *know* we'll just throw it away and never know where it goes if we don't use some system, so I want you to write down everything you spend and I'll do the same and every evening we'll go over it—

RIMS

I see a long row of pleasant evenings ahead —

BOBBY

But I mean it, dear. I've been thinking about it
all day.

RIMS

[*Definite*] Well, that part's out.

BOBBY

What part?

RIMS

[*He puts out his cigarette*] About writing it all
down. That's out. No, thanks. I knew a guy
that did that.

BOBBY

I think it's very sensible.

RIMS

[*Flaring up*] And make me accountable to you
for every cent I spend?

BOBBY

Oh, is *that* the way you look at it?

RIMS

That's what it amounts to, isn't it?

BOBBY

[*Rising*] Well, then, I guess we won't discuss the matter any further. I'll finish the dishes. [*Pause.*]

RIMS

[*Taking notebook and studying it*] No, wait a minute. There's something away out here.

BOBBY

[*Busy with the dishes*] It doesn't matter.

RIMS

Well, look here! Where do you get that two forty a month stuff? We don't get any two forty a month.

BOBBY

I've gone over and over everything.

RIMS

I know, but you're wrong. I get forty dollars a week. Four times forty's just 160 . . . [*A pause.*]

BOBBY

Oh! . . oh . . . oh, what a fool! I know what I did — but I could never tell you — I must have put down sixty a week to start — but you'd never see how I could —

RIMS

It makes a hell of a big difference, I'll say —

BOBBY

Oh, I'm such a fool.   It was just because Mengle
had spoken of a raise — and I started to figure it
on the basis of a new salary — and then I forgot
and thought I'd started with forty dollars — no,
I can't see how I did it!   [*Suddenly face to face
with it.*]   Well, then, there's just no use, you see.
We get 160 and our expenses are 174 and —

RIMS

Well, that's round numbers, you know.

BOBBY

We've just got to cut everything away down.
Rims, we can't live on 160 a month.

RIMS

Well, some months it's more.   Extra pay-days.

BOBBY

I suppose that's what's saved us so far.

RIMS

And then I'm going to get more, too, you know.

BOBBY

I hope so.

RIMS

And, I do — I do appreciate it — you're taking the trouble to figure it all out — only it's a kind of a blow too. [*He rises.*] I didn't know it was so close. Gosh, I never used to have any money troubles to speak of — I just ran along —

BOBBY

Well, so did I. I wish I hadn't quit my job.

RIMS

Well, we both couldn't work in the same office after we got married. It doesn't go somehow.

BOBBY

It would have been embarrassing, but — it wouldn't really matter.

RIMS

Well, I'd mind if you didn't. It would make it look as if I weren't man enough to — to support my wife.

BOBBY

How I hate that word.

RIMS

What word?

BOBBY

Wife! I won't be a *wife!* It sounds so fat and stupid! I wish we hadn't *got* married! I wish you'd gone to South America.

RIMS

— Well, you haven't got anything on me.

BOBBY

[*Gently*] No, I didn't mean that, dear.   It's not true.

RIMS

As a matter of fact, I meant to go to South America.

BOBBY

I know.

RIMS

And then I went to see you — and I guess I just had to have you — that's all.

BOBBY

[*Burying her head on his shoulder*] No, it was me.   I had to — have you.   It was my fault.

RIMS

[*Holding her close*] No, I knew what I was doing all right.   And hell, I — I still feel that way. You look like a million dollars to me every time I see you.

BOBBY

[*Looking up at him*] Darling, you do love me, don't you?

RIMS

Honest, kid, nobody ever loved anybody the way I love you. I'm just silly about you. I think about you all day long. And then I come home at night and — [*He turns away*] we get into some goddam mess — and it just shoots the works —

BOBBY

I know. It's just the same way with me. I think all day how marvellous it's going to be when you come home — and then you get here — and I don't know — it isn't marvellous at all — It's just a house and we're just married people — and — sometimes I hate it — everything's getting spoiled —

RIMS

I guess it's mostly relatives and — money.

BOBBY

And pipe cleaners and clothes — and meals and — dishes — oh, I haven't touched those dishes yet —

RIMS

Anyway, you're marvellous, kid. You really are.

BOBBY

Even when I'm doing dishes?

RIMS

Even when you're doing dishes. And just to prove it I'm going to help you with them.

BOBBY

I don't want you to have to do dishes.

RIMS

Gee, I wish you didn't have to.

BOBBY

I even wish you never had to see me doing dishes. I almost wish I was somebody else's wife — so you could be my lover — and come to see me when he wasn't home —

RIMS

Well, I don't know about that —

BOBBY

No, not really, I mean: but don't you see it would be better — because you'd always like me then — and you'd always want to see me and we'd have to scheme and meet places and you'd hate the old brute that owned me.

RIMS

The only trouble is I'm the old brute that owns you —

BOBBY

Only you're not an old brute — but if you were
— oh, I'd have the handsomest, dearest lover —
just like you!

RIMS

I guess you mean it for a compliment so it's all
right —

BOBBY

Oh, I do. He'd be wealthy, you see —

RIMS

Who would?

BOBBY

The brute would, and I'd have all the men in the
world to choose from — and I'd take Rims.

RIMS

If you feel that way, what do we care if we're
poor.

BOBBY

Ain't it the truth?

RIMS

[*His arms round her*] And you can lose my pipe-
cleaners and add up wrong and have relatives to
dinner and smoke my cigarettes forever and I
won't get mad.

BOBBY

I guess it was me got mad.   I always do.

RIMS

Compared to me you never get mad.

BOBBY

[*Smiling and going back to the dishes*] Only I
don't think my relatives are so very terrible, do
you?

RIMS

I guess not.   No more'n most relatives.

BOBBY

And they don't come here so very often, do they?

RIMS

Well, they were here last night.

BOBBY

Yes.

RIMS

And the night before that.   *And* the night before
that.

BOBBY

Yes, it is true.   It's partly because Florrie helped
plant the garden.

RIMS

You know the old man's all right, but that sister of yours does kind of give me the pip, and what that Willy boy ever married her for is more than I can figure out.   They actually think they own this place just because they saw it first.

BOBBY

[*Going to him*] Darling, as soon as the lease runs out we'll move.

RIMS

When do we pay the rent?

BOBBY

It's due day after tomorrow.

RIMS

Could it wait?

BOBBY

It won't have to.   With to-day's money we can just do it.

RIMS

Well, I was going to ask you — they're having a stag blow-out for old Juan — he's just back from South America and he's retiring and the boys are getting him something, chipping in, you know. Do you think I could take five out of the rent money?   It's two dollars a plate and they're chipping in about three.

BOBBY

Now, why should you give Juan anything?

RIMS

Well, he was pretty good to me, Bobby — and after the way I dropped out of the South America thing I don't want to look like a crab.

BOBBY

When is it?

RIMS

Wednesday.

BOBBY

Wednesday?   Really?

RIMS

Yeah.

BOBBY

That's funny.

RIMS

Why?

BOBBY

Guess who called me up to-day?

RIMS

Fred?

BOBBY

No. . . . Mengle.

RIMS

The boss —? What did he want?

BOBBY

Well, first he wanted to know if I'd come back and work for him —

RIMS

[*Belligerently*] Oh, he did, did he? I'd like to see you —

BOBBY

Well, I said no, and he said, " Come down and see me sometime," and I said, " All right," and he said "Why don't you come and have dinner sometime," and I said, " No, thanks," and he said, " How about Wednesday night?"

RIMS

What did you tell him?

BOBBY

I told him I'd call up and let him know.

RIMS

Why didn't you tell him to go to the devil?

BOBBY

Well, I'd been going over these figures and I thought if our income was doubled — how easy it would be — and if I just took my job back —

RIMS

Get this from me right now, kid. I won't have
you sitting in Mengle's private office taking dictation. It was bad enough before we were married.

BOBBY

Well, I guess I'll do as I please about that, my
dear.

RIMS

You will not! You'll do as I tell you.

BOBBY

[*Icily*] I might if you asked me nicely, but —

RIMS

I'm not asking you! I'm telling you, and that's
once for all! And you won't go to dinner with
him, either!

BOBBY

I didn't intend to go to dinner with him, but if
you say you won't let me, I certainly will.

RIMS

Oh, no, you won't.

BOBBY

Yes?

RIMS

Yeah, that'd put me in a nice position, wouldn't it? Me at the banquet and you dining alone with Mengle.

BOBBY

Well, I've had dinner with him before and it didn't seem to hurt your position much.

RIMS

That was before we were married!

BOBBY

Well, Good God, what's the difference?

RIMS

You know damn well what's the difference.

BOBBY

Oh dear, we're quarreling again — over nothing.

RIMS

You call that nothing! Anyway, what the hell do I care if we are? I come home here every evening just because you're here — and what thanks do I get for it? They had a game going over at Perry's and I certainly wish I'd gone.

BOBBY

I certainly wish you had. I suppose you come home every evening just to keep me company — because you're afraid I'll be lonely —

RIMS

Sometimes I do.

BOBBY

Well, go to your game.   I won't be lonely.   Any time you don't come home I can amuse myself plenty.

RIMS

All right!

BOBBY

I had a bid out myself to-night if you want to know.

RIMS

Who was it?

BOBBY

Don't you wish you knew?

RIMS

Was it Mengle?

BOBBY

No it was Fred.   He said he was all alone at the club party to-night and he wished I was going to be there.

RIMS

Are you going?

BOBBY

Why, darling, I was staying home *to keep you company*. But I wouldn't mind seeing another man once in a while — now that's the truth. [*The door-bell rings*] I wonder who that is?

RIMS

You know all right. It's that sister of yours and her Willy boy. That's who it always is.

BOBBY

Rims! [*She goes out to open the door.* RIMS *puts on his coat and drops a paper from his pocket.*]

FLORRIE

[*At the front door*] Oh, there you are. We were just going round to the back.

BOBBY

[*In the front room*] Hello, Florrie. Hello, Willy.

WILLY

[*Off*] I didn't want to come, Bobby, but she made me.

FLORRIE

[*Off*] Willy, you're making me furious!

WILLY

[*Off*] I know damn well they don't want a lot of old married folks running in on 'em at all hours.

BOBBY

[*Off*] Come on out to the kitchen — we're just finishing the dishes.   [BOBBY *re-enters, bringing* FLORRIE *and* WILLY.]

FLORRIE

Hello, Rims, darling.

RIMS

[*Over his shoulder*] Hello.

WILLY

Hello, Rims.

RIMS

Hello.

FLORRIE

Such a heavenly night you never saw!   And a lovely, lovely moon.

WILLY

That wasn't any moon.   That was a street lamp.

FLORRIE

Oh, all right, grumpie, there wasn't any moon. There, doesn't that prove I love him?   Because there really is a moon.

WILLY

There is not.

FLORRIE

I know, dear. I'm always wrong. And all the North and South streets *do* run east and west, and the sun *does* rise over New Jersey, just as you said. What did you ever marry me for if you don't like me?

WILLY

Yeah, this is a fine time to ask me that.

FLORRIE

I wish I had a perfect husband like Rims, that never got sulky. Rims, when I get my divorce, will you marry me? Shall we fly together?

RIMS

I'm going out and get some cigarets.

WILLY

Mind if I come along?

RIMS

Nope.

FLORRIE

Well say, come back after me, do you hear?

WILLY

[*Following* RIMS *out*] Yeah!

FLORRIE

Well, darling.   Did I hear sounds of family revelry, — and is the husband in a vile mood? — not really?

BOBBY

What did you hear?

FLORRIE

Only the breaking of furniture and the fall of crockery.   Who wins this evening?

BOBBY

Who wins?

FLORRIE

Why yes.   The evening row.

BOBBY

I guess neither of us won.   I guess we both lost.

FLORRIE

Then it's a draw, stupid.   Only why take it seriously.   It's the one that takes it seriously that loses.

BOBBY

It's not funny, Florrie.

FLORRIE

You child — it is funny.   You're going through a period of adjustment and it's always funny. There's a man writing for the American —

BOBBY

Yes, I know —

FLORRIE

Well, he says, there's always a period of adjustment before it's settled who's to boss the other one, and the period of adjustment is just one long series of rows.

BOBBY

I see.

FLORRIE

[*Sighing*] Willy and I are nearing the end of our period of adjustment. Willy still struggles.

BOBBY

Then — I guess I don't want to be married. If it's like that.

FLORRIE

Of course you want to be married, my dear. We all want to be married. We want somebody to take care of us. Women can talk all they please about living their own lives — I don't believe it. It's all sour grapes.

BOBBY

It isn't sour grapes with me. It — it just kills me to quarrel with him — and it's always happening! Florrie, I don't know what to do.

FLORRIE

There's nothing to do.   It's quite usual.

BOBBY

You mean people always quarrel when they're married, even when they're in love, madly in love?

FLORRIE

Well, I never knew a case where they didn't.

BOBBY

It can't be true.

FLORRIE

Naturally you don't go on being madly in love forever.   Not if you're married to the person.

BOBBY

But why?

FLORRIE

Silly, you get to know him so well and he knows you so well.   You can be sort of in love with your husband but not madly in love with him.

BOBBY

Then I don't want to be married.   Because I want to be madly in love.

FLORRIE

No doubt you wish Rims had gone to Buenos Ayres.

BOBBY

No.

FLORRIE

Well, he's yours, my dear, and he was the one you wanted, so why worry about it?

BOBBY

I know it can't go on the way it is. He'll leave me or I'll leave him — or something will happen. We want to be together and then as soon as we are together, — it's no use. [*She rises*] We always say the wrong things —

FLORRIE

Then, do you know what I think?

BOBBY

No.

FLORRIE

I think it's time for you to begin having a baby.

BOBBY

But if we don't get along together now —

FLORRIE

It makes everything different. It makes you so much more important, don't you see?

BOBBY

I don't want to be important.

FLORRIE

You want to be important to Rims, don't you?

BOBBY

Yes.

FLORRIE

Well, if you're having his baby you instantly be-
come the most important thing in the world to
him. Men are funny that way. They take so
much credit and they feel so responsible, it's pa-
thetic. So long as you don't have a baby Rims is
really free, you see — and he might get tired of
you — but just you tie him down with two or
three good fat ones — and he'll stay. Willy used
to get rebellious, but not any more. Not since
the baby.

BOBBY

But that's terrible.

FLORRIE

What is

BOBBY

To keep a man that way.

FLORRIE

It's been going on a long time, my dear. I wasn't
the first to think of it.

BOBBY

You mean that's why women have children?

FLORRIE

Why, surely.

BOBBY

But they want to have them.

FLORRIE

Oh, yes. I suppose, partly they want to keep their husbands because they want to have children, and partly they want to have children because they want to keep their husbands. Anyway, it works.

BOBBY

It wouldn't — with us.

FLORRIE

You're just like the rest of us. It's a scientific fact. It works. Some morning you'll tell Rims it's going to happen, and all of a sudden everything will change. He'll bring you things and mother you, and smother you with kisses, and he'll be humble and happy and — well, you see, there's no arguing about a thing like that —

BOBBY

Oh, but I couldn't let it happen without telling him first.

FLORRIE
Why not?

BOBBY
He might not like it.

FLORRIE
He'll like it after it happens.

BOBBY
But I couldn't.   It wouldn't be honest.

FLORRIE
Of course, he mustn't ever know it wasn't an accident.

BOBBY
We'd have to talk about it.

FLORRIE
Really.

BOBBY
Yes.

FLORRIE
Well, he'd say no, and that would be the end of that.

BOBBY
That's what I think.

FLORRIE
Unless — unless you did it — in a special way.

BOBBY

Is it another scheme?

FLORRIE

Scheme?

BOBBY

Like the — the questions on the pad?

FLORRIE

Well, didn't that one work out?

BOBBY

Yes, only I wish I'd never done it. I wish it had happened some other way.

FLORRIE

It couldn't have and you know it. Wait till some time when he's just crazy about you — you know — and then say —

BOBBY

Don't say it, *please!*

FLORRIE

If you think he'd see through it, dear, you're wrong. It's appalling what they never see through.

BOBBY

Oh, I wish we hadn't talked about it!

FLORRIE

Well, it may not be necessary yet. But any time you're really afraid of losing him, I'd say — [*The door bell rings.* BOBBY *goes into the living room to answer it.*]

FLORRIE

Well, I've got to go anyway.

MR. HALEVY

[*In the living room*] Just the old man.

BOBBY

[*Still outside*] Oh, hello, Dad!   I couldn't think who it would be — Where's mother?   [FLORRIE *rises, finds on the floor the paper* RIMS *dropped from his pocket, and reads it.*]

MR. HALEVY

[*Outside*] She was tired.   She went to bed early.

BOBBY

[*Outside*] Come on out.   Florrie's here.

MR. HALEVY

[*Entering*] Hello, Florrie.   [BOBBY *enters behind him.*]

FLORRIE

Hello, grandfather.

MR. HALEVY

Shut up that grandfather stuff!

FLORRIE

[*In her sweetest baby talk*] Why, you precious old dear, are you ashamed of being a grand-father?

MR. HALEVY

Wait till you're a grandmother, and you'll know how I feel. If there's anything more humiliating than having squalling children it's having squal-ling grand-children.

FLORRIE

But he doesn't squall!

MR. HALEVY

Of course not. He *coos*.

FLORRIE

He's really a love, daddy. Imagine your never coming to see him! Not that I mind really. Bobby, I'll have to run along without Willy. You can tell him when he comes back. Some-thing I found on the floor. [*She hands* BOBBY *the paper.*]

BOBBY

[*Laying it down*] Thanks, — I'm sorry you have to go.

FLORRIE

You'd better look at that. It's an I. O. U. Somebody owes Rims some money.

BOBBY

[*Looking at the thing*] Owes Rims money?

FLORRIE

Well, it's an I. O. U.

BOBBY

Oh.

FLORRIE

Don't let the boy gamble, dear. Well, goodbye.
Why don't you come over sometime? We always come to see you and you never come to see
us.

BOBBY

We will, Florrie, goodbye. [FLORRIE *goes.*]

MR. HALEVY

[*Lighting a cigar*] Well, kiddie, how's things?

BOBBY

Dad, what's an I. O. U. for?

MR. HALEVY

You mean you don't know?

BOBBY

I knew people gave them — but how would
Rims happen to have one.

MR. HALEVY

I'd say he's lucky — if it's any good.

BOBBY

He couldn't have lent anybody money — because he didn't have it to lend.

MR. HALEVY

Then he won it.

BOBBY

But he didn't tell me.

MR. HALEVY

Why should he tell you everything, child? Do you think you own the boy just because he's married to you?

BOBBY

But it's for twenty-seven dollars, and to think of his not saying a word about it and we've been talking budget all evening —

MR. HALEVY

Well, ask him, ask him.

BOBBY

Dad —

MR. HALEVY

Yes?

BOBBY

Do you think — ? I don't know —

MR. HALEVY

All right — what's on your mind?

BOBBY

Do you think — I ought to have a baby? [*A pause*]

MR. HALEVY

[*A whisper*] What!

BOBBY

Do you think I ought to have a baby? [MR. HALEVY *looks at her — then looks away and smiles.*]

MR. HALEVY

Jesus look down! How old are you, girlie?

BOBBY

Please don't be foolish.

MR. HALEVY

Yes, I suppose you are old enough. That was the wrong thing to say. But looking back at my beautiful wasted youth — why anybody should want to have a baby — why anybody should even want to get married — is more than — I can ever understand. — From me, my dear, I fear you will get nothing but ribald advice and evil counselling. I'd better go home.

BOBBY

No, don't go. This is serious!

MR. HALEVY

Bobby. I married young and brought up two lovely children. I can't say I regret it, but there are moments, and those moments occur more frequently now that I'm a grandfather, when it appears to me that Don Juan and Casanova chose the better part.

BOBBY

Yes, I suppose that's true if you're a man, but I'm not.

MR. HALEVY

I used to wish you were.

BOBBY

Why?

MR. HALEVY

Now, don't ask me to talk seriously on this topic, my dear. After all, I'm your father and I know my duty. If I said, " No, don't have any babies," you'd ask me if I was sorry we had you and Florrie, and I couldn't think of an adequate reply. Anyway, fathers shouldn't confide in their daughters. It isn't hundred per cent —. No

doubt it would be considered a kind of intellec-
tual incest.   But I can tell you lies by the yard —

BOBBY

Then you think having a baby — would be a
mistake?

MR. HALEVY

I didn't even want you to get married.

BOBBY

You didn't say anything —

MR. HALEVY

I came near it — the night you and Rims fixed it
up.   I was afraid it was going to happen.

BOBBY

Oh.

MR. HALEVY

Do you know how fathers feel about their
daughters when they're growing up?

BOBBY

No.

MR. HALEVY

Well, they think — when they think about it —
here I have two good-looking virtuous girls, and
I'm putting in my whole life raising them up,

feeding them, sending them to school — and for what? All for the service and delight of two unknown and probably disagreeable young men. So I used to wish I had sons, because they could have a good time at any rate. And then it occurred to me there was no reason why girls shouldn't have a good time.

BOBBY

How do you mean?

MR. HALEVY

Fall in love — have your affair — and when it's over — get out!

BOBBY

Oh!

MR. HALEVY

I told you I'd better go home.

BOBBY

But why not have a love affair — and get married?

MR. HALEVY

Marriage is no love affair, my dear. It's little old last year's love affair. It's a house and bills and dishpans and family quarrels. That's the way the system beats you. They bait the wedding with a romance and they hang a three-hundred-pound landlord around your neck and drown you in grocery bills. If I'd talked to you that night I'd have said — if you're in love with him, why have your affair, sow a few oats. Why the devil should the boys have a monopoly on wild oats?

BOBBY

Yes, I see.

MR. HALEVY

No, I shouldn't say that. Marriage is fine, kiddie, it's grand. It's the corner stone of progress. It's the backbone of civilization. Don't you believe anything against it.

BOBBY

Please, dad.

MR. HALEVY

But if I had talked to you that night, I'd have said, you're too young to get married. You haven't had any fun yet. He hasn't money enough to support you. Why should he support you? You're his economic equal.

BOBBY

Maybe I should have gone on working.

MR. HALEVY

Yes, and if you had gone on working and he
didn't support you, why take his name and label
yourself? I don't see it. . . . No, I shouldn't
talk that way. I take it back.

BOBBY

I might have lost him.

MR. HALEVY

Not so surely as you'll lose him now. It used to
be a love affair, didn't it?

BOBBY

Yes.

MR. HALEVY

What is it, as is?

BOBBY

Grocery bills — mostly.

MR. HALEVY

I'm — I'm sorry.

BOBBY

Then — then why didn't mother lose you?

MR. HALEVY

Well, maybe she did. And maybe I lost her. Of
course we stayed around. We had children.

BOBBY

And — didn't you like having children?

MR. HALEVY

Now, to be honest — children do get you — they do get you. I have to admit that, — and I suppose a man wants to have children — just to prove he's all right. Before you have children you're afraid something's the matter with you — yes, and after you have them, you're sure of it. But — you don't go away. You see, you start one baby, just as a kind of experiment, and then you find it's a life sentence. [*Pause*] For both of you.

BOBBY

But — if you have a husband — and you want to keep him all your life long — then maybe a baby is the best thing — isn't it?

MR. HALEVY

You scheming little devil!

BOBBY

It's true, isn't it?

MR. HALEVY

Oh, yes, it'll hold him, and you too.

BOBBY

You don't understand me, dad. I'm young and foolish — and Rims is everything in the world to me and I'm afraid I'll lose him. I can't help being young and foolish. [*The door bell rings.*]

MR. HALEVY

No, I suppose not.

BOBBY

So I guess I'll make it — a life sentence.

MR. HALEVY

All right. — Only think it over. [*The bell rings again.* BOBBY *goes out to the door.*]

FLORRIE

[*Outside*] Hello, Bobby. It's only us again.

BOBBY

Why Florrie, come in.

FLORRIE

I just happened to meet Willy and he said he had a message for you. [*She enters, followed by* BOBBY *and* WILLY.] That is, Rims asked him to tell you he'd be home late.

BOBBY

Oh. Oh, yes.

WILLY

Why, you see, he got a chance to get into a little game, so he told me to tell you to look for him when you saw him coming —

BOBBY

Oh.

FLORRIE

Never mind, dear. They all get that way sometimes. Give him rope.

WILLY

Sure, give him plenty of rope. That's always the best plan. And, by the way, Florrie, I may be out late tomorrow night. Don't look for me —

FLORRIE

No, you don't, darling.

WILLY

I thought not.

FLORRIE

Why, Willy, you know you always go out when you really want to —

WILLY

Well, as I often say, I wouldn't have known it if you hadn't told me.

BOBBY

[*In her father's arms*] Dad!

MR. HALEVY

It's all right, dear.

BOBBY

I — I don't think he likes me any more.

MR. HALEVY

Sure, he likes you. He'd better like you, or I'd horsewhip him. Upstart cub!

BOBBY

Oh, no, dad, he's —

MR. HALEVY

I'd like to know what he's ever done to deserve a girl like my Bobby.

BOBBY

No, — I'm not good enough for him, dad — you don't know him. — [RIMS *enters by the back door.*]

MR. HALEVY

I don't have to know him.

FLORRIE

Why, Rims — Hello!

RIMS

[*Crossing to the living room*] Hello.

FLORRIE

Well, can we do anything for you, Rims? Kill a fatted calf, or something? [*There is no answer. A chair falls over, and a pile of books slide to the floor.*]

RIMS

[*In living room*] God damn it!

BOBBY

[*Going to the door*] Can't I help you?

RIMS

No.

BOBBY

[*Going into the living room*] There's nothing in that closet but your overcoat —

RIMS

I'm just looking for something.

BOBBY

All right. [*She re-enters and picks up the I. O. U. RIMS comes in, evidently hunting for something.*] Were you looking for this, Rims?

RIMS

Where was it?

BOBBY

Why —

RIMS

Yeah, I know damn well where it was and so do you! It was in my coat pocket!

BOBBY

Maybe it was. I don't know.

RIMS

I'll bet you don't.

FLORRIE

Why, Rims, darling, what a thing to say to little wifie!

RIMS

[*Turning on her*] Baby talk!

FLORRIE

And I suppose you never talk baby talk.

RIMS

No!

MR. HALEVY

[*Turning to leave*] It was on the floor, Rims. You ought to take better care of your valuable papers. Well, Bobby, I'll be running along. [*He goes.*]

RIMS

Oh, stay! Spend the night! I'm going.

FLORRIE

What a charming manner he has with guests.

WILLY

[*Going out*] Keep out of it, can't you? It's none of your affair.

FLORRIE

Bobby, I'll run along! And Rims, you're just a love, just a perfect love. [*She goes out.*]

RIMS

Yeah, I always liked you too! You've got a grand family, take it all round . . . can't understand why your mother wasn't here . . . well. So long. [*He crosses to the door, then pauses.*] You probably want to know where I got that I. O. U.

BOBBY

[*Looking away*] No.

RIMS

Well, I'll tell you anyway. I got it playing blackjack. I guess I've got a right to a game even if I am married . . . you don't need to look so tragic. I always played cards and I'll do it some more.

BOBBY

I don't mind anything except you said you needed money — and you had some.

RIMS

Sure. I know. You think you've got a mortgage on everything I get. . . . That's why you want me to write it down on a book. So you won't miss anything.

BOBBY

Why do you have to be nasty about it?

RIMS

I'm not being nasty. I'm telling you a few things. You do as you please, you go to dinner with Mengle, you take back your job with him and as good as tell me if I don't like it I can go chase myself. Well then, by God, I'll do as I please. . . . Anyway, I didn't get that twenty-seven free and clear. I got an I. O. U. for 27 and I gave one for 29. I was two dollars in the hole . . . I didn't tell you because I didn't want to . . . I'm not used to telling anybody everything.

BOBBY

Well, don't worry about it, dear. Run along, and have a good time —

RIMS

You know, I haven't got anything against you — only I'm just not used to it, that's all. — I guess it's all right. I'm the earning end and you're the paying end and we've got to work together. Only it comes kind of hard. . . .

BOBBY

It surely comes hard to me, Rims.

RIMS

Aw, I'm not going. [*He throws his hat on a chair.*]

BOBBY

Why not? Run along. Have a good time.

RIMS

How can I have a good time — if you don't say goodbye to me?

BOBBY

Goodbye.

RIMS

Ah, kid . . . kiss me goodbye. [*She is silent. He turns again.*]

BOBBY

Rims! [*He drops his hat again and she throws herself into his arms.*]

RIMS

You know, I think it's that sister of yours. Every time she comes in the house, I see red. I don't like your family. That's the truth.

BOBBY

I wish I didn't have any family. I wish there was just you and me —

RIMS

Everybody ought to be born orphans.

BOBBY

Rims, do you really like me, or are you just being kind to me?

RIMS

You know darn well I'm crazy about you. But, hell, the way everybody goes blooey —

BOBBY

Well then I don't care how things go.

RIMS

[*Holding her*] Sweetheart! . . . Well, I guess I ought to be getting along, kid. The fellows are waiting for me.

BOBBY

Don't — don't go quite yet —

RIMS

All right.

BOBBY

Don't you think, there must be something wrong, dear? Or else we'd be happier?

RIMS

I don't know. We're pretty happy.

BOBBY

No, — no, we're not.

RIMS

Well, maybe you're right.

BOBBY

Maybe — maybe we ought to have a baby.

RIMS

Good God, girl! I guess we've got trouble enough — you think I want to join the chain gang? A baby! Say, did you ever see a kid you didn't want to run from?

BOBBY

I just thought maybe — we'd like each other better —

RIMS

For the love of Mike! . . . Say, kid, are you — ? Are you?

BOBBY

No; oh, no!

RIMS

Well, I'm glad of that. That would — make it different.

BOBBY

Would it, dear?

RIMS

Would it?

BOBBY

Rims — if you knew what I wanted, more than anything else, would you let me have it?

RIMS

I guess it — it would depend.

BOBBY

Rims, dear, when a woman's truly in love with a man — and believes in him, why then what she wants most of anything — is to have a baby with him — a baby that would be just ours —

RIMS

Why, darling — gosh, kid — why — you see, we couldn't afford — say, I didn't know you felt that way — but if you — if you do —

BOBBY

No, I can't do it! I can't go through with it!

RIMS

What do you mean?

BOBBY

[*Turning on him*] What do I mean? I was roping you in. That's what I mean — and I can't do
it! I was afraid I might lose you, that's all, and I
thought I could keep you if we — if there was
a —

RIMS

Oh, you were roping me in?

BOBBY

Yes, but I won't do it. I won't keep you that
way. If I can't keep you on the level, why, I'll
just have to lose you —

RIMS

I see.

BOBBY

Because — I love you too much —

RIMS

Did somebody put you up to that or did you
invent it for yourself?

BOBBY

No.

RIMS

No what?

BOBBY

I just — thought of it.

RIMS

No you didn't. It's not like you. Somebody put you up to it.

BOBBY

Well, forget it. — I've been keeping you —

RIMS

[*Fiercely*] If it was that sister of yours —

BOBBY

Well, what if it was? I'm being honest with you now anyway. I'm going to be so honest it hurts. It isn't the first time I tried to trick you. I tricked you into marrying me.

RIMS

When?

BOBBY

When you asked me to marry you. Didn't you see it?

RIMS

No.

BOBBY

Well, it was obvious enough.

RIMS

Did she put you up to that too?

BOBBY

It doesn't matter. I did it.

RIMS

All right, I've got her number. And yours too.
It's the last time you put anything over on me —

BOBBY

I don't want to put anything over on you. If
I'd wanted to. I could have, couldn't I? — and I
didn't!

RIMS

Listen, kid — I think we're going to have a show-
down right here and now! A fellow gives up a
lot when he gets married. As long as he's single,
he owns the earth, but when he's married his
money's not his own, his time's not his own, he's
got to keep on working whether he wants to or
not, and there's hell to pay if he spends an extra
dime. Whenever I tired of my job I used to quit
— if I didn't like one town I tried another —
and now I can't —

BOBBY

Why not?

RIMS

Because I've got a wife — because I've got a family?

BOBBY

Good God — am I a family? I won't be a wife — I won't be a family! I'm just me!

RIMS

All right, be yourself!

BOBBY

All right, I'll be myself — and if you think a man gives up a lot when he gets married, a girl gives up something when she gets married, and don't you forget it! I spend the whole day here taking care of this damned house for you and cooking your meals and washing your dishes and never going anywhere because we can't afford it — and every time I get a dime for myself I have to ask for it! It's degrading!

RIMS

It's your own home.

BOBBY

It's not mine. It's all yours. You earn the money so it's all yours! I tell you it's despicable! Asking!

RIMS

Throw it up to me I don't earn enough!   That's right!

BOBBY

Well, you don't!

RIMS

You knew how much I was earning when you married me.   If you don't like it, why see what you can do about it!

BOBBY

Oh!   Oh!   Well I know what I can do about it!

RIMS

Well, you won't work for Mengle!   If it's my house I'm going to have my way in it, and I won't have my wife working for Mengle!   I give up a good deal to keep this damn place going and it's going to be the way I want it from now on —

BOBBY

Oh, it will!   Well, I still know my way to the front door!   I guess I know when I've got enough!   [*She goes into front room.*]

RIMS

Where are you going?   [BOBBY *stops in the arch, turns, and faces him.*]

BOBBY

[*Screaming*] You can wash your own dishes! The hot water's in the right hand tap! I'm running along! And I'm not coming back! [*She storms out.*]

RIMS

[*Calling*] You mean you're leaving me?

BOBBY

[*In the living room*] If you don't believe it, you watch me!

RIMS

[*Picking up his hat and coat*] All right. Suits me. Two can play at that game. I'm not stopping you. Got any money?

BOBBY

[*Re-entering with her coat and hat on*] I've got the rent money.

RIMS

If you go to work for Mengle I quit him!

BOBBY

[*Picking up her pocket book*] I don't care where you work. It's a free country. Goodbye. [*She goes out through the living room; the door slams.*]

RIMS

Goodbye. [*He goes out the back door, slam-
ming it. After a moment he comes in, shaken
and humbled.*] Bobby! [*There is no answer.
He turns off the kitchen light and goes out. The
light in the living room still burns.* BOBBY *comes
back through the living room.*]

BOBBY

Rims! Rims, dear! [*No answer. She turns
slowly, crosses to the living room and goes out
again, switching off the light. The front door
closes.*]

CURTAIN

ACT THREE

Three weeks later.
A bedroom in MRS. GORLIK'S *boarding house in
East 33rd St.*
*There is an entrance door at the left, a closet at
the right.   Near the closet an open window re-
veals a moonlit night and a fire-escape.   There
are a couple of ancient chairs, a dresser and an
iron bed.   The paper on the wall has been there
— well, as long as the carpet on the floor.*
*The stage is altogether dark save for the light
outside the window.   A breeze blows the curtains
gently.*   [*There is a knock at the door.*]

MRS. GORLIK

[*Outside*] Are you in yet, miss? [*She enters,
switches on the lights and goes across to close
the window, muttering.*]   Never knew a girl
wasn't a born fool.   Leaves her window up with
all these robberies — gets all my curtains dirty
— [*She inspects a pair of stockings drying
on a towel rack.*]   T'ain't decent! [*A door bell
rings below.*] [*She looks at the second pair.*] Another pair.

A VOICE

[*From the basement*] Mrs. Gorlik!

MRS. GORLIK

What do you want?

VOICE

[*From basement*] Man on his way up to see Miss
Halevy.

MRS. GORLIK

What?

VOICE

Man here to see Miss Halevy.

MRS. GORLIK

She ain't here.

VOICE

He's on his way up.

MRS. GORLIK

Well, tell him the second floor.

VOICE

Second floor, mister!

MR. HALEVY

[*On the stairs*] Looking for Miss Halevy's room.

MRS. GORLIK

This is her room, but I don't know when she'll
be in.

MR. HALEVY

[*Entering*] That's all right, I'll just wait for her. I suppose I can wait for her?

MRS. GORLIK

You mean you'll wait here?

MR. HALEVY

Well not necessarily here — if you'd rather I waited somewhere else.

MRS. GORLIK

I don't know when she's coming back, and I don't know as you'd better wait.

MR. HALEVY

What's that?

MRS. GORLIK

I said, I don't know as you'd better wait.

MR. HALEVY

Well you see I always decide these matters for myself, my dear Miss —

MRS. GORLIK

[*Positive*] Mrs. Gorlik.

MR. HALEVY

Yes. Well you see, Mrs. Gorlik, I'm Miss Halevy's father. Now, if you'd rather I waited in the parlor —

MRS. GORLIK

There ain't any parlor.

MR. HALEVY

[*Smiling*] Don't apologize, Mrs. Gorlik.   And don't worry about me.   I'm perfectly all right.

MRS. GORLIK

Well, if you're her father —

MR. HALEVY

I am.

MRS. GORLIK

Then I should say it's a very good thing you came.

MR. HALEVY

Yes?   [*He takes out his pipe.*]

MRS. GORLIK

Because she needs looking after.

MR. HALEVY

You don't say.

MRS. GORLIK

[*Seeing his pipe*] You can't smoke here, you know.   Not a pipe.

MR. HALEVY

I beg your pardon.   And so you think she needs looking after?

MRS. GORLIK

She certainly does.

MR. HALEVY

What makes you think so?

MRS. GORLIK

I can tell. When they come here looking for rooms late at night and when they have middle-aged gentlemen to call like she done last night — and when they smoke cigarettes — well — I can tell. [*The door-bell again.*]

MR. HALEVY

Then you — you won't mind if I wait —

VOICE

[*From the basement*] Mrs. Gorlik.

MRS. GORLIK

What do you want?

VOICE

Another gentleman to see Miss Halevy.

MRS. GORLIK

I'll be right down! [*She goes out.*]

VOICE

He's coming up!

MRS. GORLIK

[*Outside*] Are you the gentleman to see Miss Halevy?

RIMS

[*Outside*] Miss Halevy hell, I'm here to see Mrs. O'Neil. [*He enters and sees* MR. HALEVY.]

MRS. GORLIK

There ain't any Mrs. O'Neil here.   And besides — [*She stops, seeing they know each other.*]

MR. HALEVY

Hello, Rims.

RIMS

Hello. [Mrs. Gorlik goes.]

MR. HALEVY

Bobby coming in soon?

RIMS

I don't know.

MR. HALEVY

Because if she is I'll run along. I didn't know you two'd got together.

RIMS

Me? I haven't seen her.

MR. HALEVY

Oh, I see.

RIMS

Yeah. I came in on the chance she might be here.

MR. HALEVY

So did I.

RIMS

You know when I first came in, I thought you were Mengle.

MR. HALEVY

Well, how is Mengle for looks?

RIMS

I'm no judge. I hate the face off him.

MR. HALEVY

What made you think he might be here?

RIMS

That's all right.

MR. HALEVY

Maybe you under-estimate Bobby.

RIMS

You think so?

MR. HALEVY

Or, maybe I under-estimate you. What made you think Mengle might be here? — [RIMS *doesn't answer.*] All right!

RIMS

[*Rising*] Listen, do you think I've been having an easy time these last three weeks?

MR. HALEVY

I don't know.

RIMS

Maybe you think I've been having the time of
my life. My wife's left me. Now's my chance
to step out, I suppose — why not? She does.

MR. HALEVY

That's funny!

RIMS

Yeah!

MR. HALEVY

Because if there was any one thing in the world
she wanted it was you.

RIMS

How do you know?

MR. HALEVY

I know.

RIMS

Listen, Mr. Halevy. I called her up. She said
I can't see her. Then I tried having some fun,
but it wasn't any good. I don't want to play
cards. I don't want anything else in the world
except her. And — she's gone. She doesn't
need me. She's having a good time.

MR. HALEVY

You'll have to prove that to me.

RIMS

Prove it! I hung around the office last night. I
had to see her. And what happened? She comes
out with Mengle — and they went to dinner together — Jeez —

MR. HALEVY

Well — ?

RIMS

Well — She didn't see me. So I followed them.
And after dinner she let him bring her home.
He brought her here in a private car — with a
chauffeur. I guess that's what she wants. I
don't earn enough. She's got to have a private
car — with a chauffeur.

MR. HALEVY

Oh, no — no — no.

RIMS

Well, anyway, I waited outside. And pretty
soon he went away. God, I don't know what's
the matter with me. I used to have a little sense.
About girls, anyway. Now I act like a damn
dummy. You don't know what it's like!

MR. HALEVY

Don't I?

RIMS

Does everybody go crazy this way?

MR. HALEVY

[*Lighting his pipe*] Every last one of us.

RIMS

You know, when I came in and thought Mengle was here, I was going to beat him up.

MR. HALEVY

No, no — that wouldn't do any good, you know.

RIMS

No.   But it'd be a lot of fun.

MR. HALEVY

You're lucky, Rims.   You young fellows don't know how lucky you are.   When a man's young he makes love — when he's middle-aged he makes money — or tries to — and when he's old he makes his soul.   I never could make any money to speak of, so I suppose it's about time I began to make my soul.   But I'd rather be young — and make love to a girl that was in love with me.   There's nothing like it.

RIMS

She's not in love with me, Mr. Halevy. That's the hell of it. If she were, she wouldn't have gone away.

MR. HALEVY

Well, you went away, too, didn't you? And you were in love with her?

RIMS

Yeah. But —

MR. HALEVY

Maybe she left you because she was in love with you. [RIMS, *more or less taken aback at this idea, pauses for a moment, then reaches for his hat.*] Where are you going, Rims?

RIMS

I'm going to take a walk around the block. [*He starts to the door and meets a chauffeur who is carrying a package.*]

THE CHAUFFEUR

I've got a package for Miss Halevy.

RIMS

You mean Mrs. O'Neil. She's not here.

THE CHAUFFEUR

They said the second floor.

RIMS

Yes, this is her room, but she's not here.   Anything I can do for you?

THE CHAUFFEUR

No.   This thing's got to be delivered personally.

RIMS

Then I guess you'll have to come back.

THE CHAUFFEUR

Yeah?

RIMS

Yeah!

THE CHAUFFEUR

[*He disappears*] All right!

RIMS

Now what the hell is going on?

MR. HALEVY

What do you think?

RIMS

Well, that's Mengle's chauffeur, isn't it?   Must deliver to her personally.   What the hell does that make me?   [*He starts to go.*]

MR. HALEVY

Wait a minute!   Shall I tell her you were here?

RIMS

No! [*He goes, bumping into* MRS. GORLIK. *She holds the door open.*]

MRS. GORLIK

You'll have to leave the door open, young man, [*She follows him down the hall and calls.*] Matty!

THE VOICE

Yes Ma'am! [MR. HALEVY *puffs vigorously on pipe*]

MRS. GORLIK

[*Outside*] See that that door is closed after that young man leaves. All the draughts in these halls is — [MRS. GORLIK *enters left*] You'll have to leave the door open with gentlemen call — [*Seeing that* BOBBY *is not there*] Oh, she ain't come in yet?

MR. HALEVY

[*Hiding the pipe*] No!

MRS. GORLIK

And the young man didn't wait?

MR. HALEVY

No!

MRS. GORLIK

You'll have to excuse me opening the door. It's not one of the things I like to do — going around opening girls' doors with gentlemen calling, Mr. Halevy. It is Mr. Halevy, ain't it?

MR. HALEVY

It is.

MRS. GORLIK

But I have to do it, much as I don't like to. [*Noticing he has sat down she does the same on edge of bed.*] If I was ever going into this business again, I wouldn't take girls, only gentlemen. True, gentlemen do get drunk and smash things. But I will say this for them. They do know how to take care of themselves, and you don't have to watch them.

MR. HALEVY

Why do you have to watch the girls?

MRS. GORLIK

[*Turning to him, breathless*] Why, my dear Mr. — Well — if you knew the kind of goings on, and what was thought of girls that close their doors with gentlemen callers — well, you wouldn't want it said about your daughter.

MR. HALEVY

You mean they get drunk and break things?
[*The door-bell rings.*]

MRS. GORLIK

I guess you know what I mean, all right.

THE VOICE

Mrs. Gorlik —

MRS. GORLIK

[*Rising*] Well what is it?

THE VOICE

There's a special delivery letter.

MRS. GORLIK

Well, sign for it. Oh, never mind, I'm coming
right down. [MR. HALEVY *resumes his pipe.*]

BOBBY

[*Outside*] Hello, Mrs. Gorlik.

MRS. GORLIK

[*Outside*] How do you do? There's a gentleman
to see you that says he's your father. [BOBBY
enters. MR. HALEVY *rises.*]

BOBBY

[*Kissing him*] Dad! Hello!

MR. HALEVY

Well, darling, I stayed away as long as I could.

BOBBY

[*Closing the door*] I'm glad you came. Do you
like my place?

MR. HALEVY

It certainly looks familiar.

BOBBY

You don't mean it looks like home?

MR. HALEVY

No. But I lived in a lot of places like this before
I was married. They haven't changed the carpet
on the stairs of any one of them.

BOBBY

It must be different, though.

MR. HALEVY

My dear, there's nothing new about these places
except the girls and boys that live in them —
But, I'm certainly not crazy about this.

BOBBY

Well, I'm not either. But they won't take girls
many places and I liked their scale of prices.
[*She hangs up her coat.*]

MR. HALEVY

You know, I walked past that little house of
yours this afternoon, and it looked pretty lonely.

And I felt pretty lonely, and I thought three weeks of this was about enough. So I decided to come over and ask you what about it.

BOBBY

Well, I wanted to be alone, and I have been.

MR. HALEVY

You know, you could have your old room — at home — any time?

BOBBY

Dad, I'll never go home. It would be like going around in a circle. I'd be right back where I started.

MR. HALEVY

I'm afraid it was partly my fault.

BOBBY

No. I did it all with my little hatchet. I cannot tell a lie. I've gone back to work, dad — and I'm living here.

MR. HALEVY

What about poor Rims?

BOBBY

What about poor me? I had to be alone, dad! I didn't dare see Rims. If I had I might have gone back to him — and then — well, we'd be right back where we were. [*A knock at the door*, BOBBY *opens it.*]

RIMS

[*Entering*] Hello!

BOBBY

Hello, Rims!

MR. HALEVY

Good evening.

RIMS

Good evening, sir.

MR. HALEVY

Don't you sir me, young man. I'm only twice your age and I don't look that. And boy, do you want to meet a nice girl? My daughter, Mr. O'Neil. A working girl, but she has class. She — [*He stops, crosses to the door, and goes out.*]

RIMS

I guess you didn't want me to find you.

BOBBY

Oh, I don't mind.

RIMS

Well, I'll tell you about that first, so you'll know how it happened. I didn't ask anybody where your room was. I followed you home last night.

BOBBY

Followed me? I had dinner with Mengle.

RIMS

I know you did. Christ, kid, I've been out of my head. I hung around the office last night to see you, and who did you come out with?

BOBBY

You waited — at the office?

RIMS

Yes —

BOBBY

I didn't see you!

RIMS

And then he came home with you. He even stayed around a while.

BOBBY

I was just lonely.

RIMS

You didn't look very lonely to me. I can't stand that. After all, you are my wife.

BOBBY

Oh, was that why you came?

RIMS

No, it wasn't. I wanted to see you. You managed to make it lovely for me!

BOBBY

Did you come to see me or did you come to lecture me about Mengle?

RIMS

Well — you had dinner with him, didn't you?

BOBBY

It was just Mengle, wasn't it? That was all you wanted to see me about?

RIMS

No, it wasn't.

BOBBY

Then — what was it?

RIMS

Oh, I guess it does not matter.

BOBBY

That's what does matter.

RIMS

Yeah?

BOBBY

Don't you think so?

RIMS

I don't know.

BOBBY

[*Sitting down*] You might — have a chair.

RIMS

[*He sits*] Thanks.

BOBBY

You have a new job I hear.

RIMS

Yeah!

BOBBY

How's it going?

RIMS

Pretty well.

BOBBY

Oh.

RIMS

Well — not bad!

BOBBY

Jobs are all pretty much alike.

RIMS

Sure.

BOBBY

What — what business is it?

RIMS

Automatic mooring winches.

BOBBY

Oh.   Oh, yes! — Are there many of them used?

RIMS

What?

BOBBY

These —

RIMS

Automatic mooring winches?

BOBBY

Yes —

RIMS

You'd be surprised. . . .   Same salary.

BOBBY

Truly?

RIMS

Yes.

BOBBY

Why that's marvellous, Rims — to change jobs
and get the same salary the first thing.   It is —
marvellous.

RIMS

Not a very nice place, is it?

BOBBY

It's inexpensive.

RIMS

It ought to be.

BOBBY

You don't like it?

RIMS

Well, you're here, of course.

BOBBY

Thanks, Rims.

RIMS

[*Rising*] Say, Bobby —

BOBBY

[*Rising, and putting the chair between them*] Yes — ?

RIMS

Are you really as hard-hearted as — as all this kind of implies?

BOBBY

When was I ever hard-hearted?

RIMS

You know, I came over here all primed to say something, and I'm damned if I know how to say it.

BOBBY

What was it?

RIMS

I came to ask you — if you hadn't had enough of it — and — maybe you'd come home now —

BOBBY

Back to the house?

RIMS

Where else?

BOBBY

No.

RIMS

What are we going to do with the house, then?

BOBBY

I guess Florrie and Willy are going to take it off our hands.

RIMS

What are you going to do?

BOBBY

Live here.

RIMS

And what am I going to do?

BOBBY

I don't know. [*There is a knock*] Come in.
[*She opens the door and finds the chauffeur with
his package.*]

THE CHAUFFEUR

I've a package for you, Miss Halevy.

BOBBY

Oh! thank you. [*She takes it.*]

THE CHAUFFEUR

You're welcome! [*He goes.* BOBBY *closes the
door.*]

RIMS

So, it's flowers Mengle's sending you, huh? Well,
you better open it.

BOBBY

I don't want to.

RIMS

Sure, open it. Why ruin the flowers — just on
my account.

BOBBY

It isn't flowers!

RIMS

Then what is it?

BOBBY

[*Opening it*] It's really something for Mrs. Gorlik.

RIMS

It's a bolt! —

BOBBY

[*Laughing*] Yes — for the door!

RIMS

[*Taking out a screw driver and a hammer*] And a hammer, and a screw driver to put it on with.

BOBBY

Well — he said he was going to send me a bolt — but I thought he was joking. You see, when Mengle was here last night, the landlady seemed to think he was a shady character and kept opening the door all the time —

RIMS

Hey! Wait a minute! Let me get this straight!

BOBBY

I suppose he thought it would be funny. And I really did want a bolt.

RIMS

Yeah, go right ahead and explain. You're making it better all the time.

BOBBY

Rims —

RIMS

Yeah, explain some more! Did you ask him for it?

BOBBY

I didn't tell him he couldn't send it.

RIMS

Oh, you didn't? Well, all right —

BOBBY

You mean you think I haven't any right to let Mr. Mengle send me a bolt for my door?

RIMS

I mean it looks damned funny to me, and it is damned funny!

BOBBY

Certainly it's funny! That's why he did it? Don't you see?

RIMS

Do I see? I'll say I see! [*He starts for the door.*]

BOBBY

[*Stepping in front of him*] Rims, if you go now, it's the last you see of me as long as you live. [*There is a pause.*]

RIMS

Well, what I can't understand is why you'd let Mengle come to your room.

BOBBY

Well, why not, if I feel like it?   It's my room. I can take care of myself.

RIMS

I doubt it.

BOBBY

Listen, Rims.   I did want you to come.   I've been waiting for you to come.   But if you're going to begin to tell me what I can do and what I can't do —

RIMS

If you don't know enough to keep clear of Mengle, you shouldn't be at large.

BOBBY

That's just the point.   I do know enough to keep clear of Mengle.   Only I'm on my own now, and I'm going to use my own judgment.

RIMS

Such as it is.

BOBBY

Exactly. Such as it is. You use yours such as it
is, and you haven't any guardian.

RIMS

What's the idea, anyway.

BOBBY

The idea is, I'm a free agent. Just as free as you
are.

RIMS

You don't care about me any more?

BOBBY

Yes, I do.

RIMS

Well, it's all right about Mengle. I can see how
it was.

BOBBY

It did look queer, I know.

RIMS

Only any time you want a bolt on your door, I
wish you'd ask me.

BOBBY

I will — if you're around.

RIMS

You know damn well I'd be around if I thought you wanted me.

BOBBY

[*Smiling*] Well, I wasn't sure you would.

RIMS

[*Coming close to* BOBBY] Listen, dear — about that house!   That isn't a bad little house — as houses go.

BOBBY

Any house is bad enough.

RIMS

[*Pleading*] You won't try it again?

BOBBY

No. . . .   You see — Oh, I wonder if I can tell you — What we wanted was a love affair, wasn't it?   Just to be together and let the rest go hang — and what we got was a house and bills and general hell.   Do you know what I think a love affair is, Rims?   It's when the whole world is trying to keep two people apart — and they insist on being together.   And when they get married the whole world pushes them together so they just naturally fly apart.   I want my love

affair back. I wanted hurried kisses and clandes-
tine meetings, and a secret lover. I don't want
a house. I don't want a husband. I want a
lover.

RIMS

So that let's me out.

BOBBY

Does it, dear? [*A knock. The door opens and*
MRS. GORLIK *appears*]

MRS. GORLIK

You'll have to leave the door open with gentlemen callers.

BOBBY

Oh, yes, Rims. I forgot to tell you. The door
should be open.

MRS. GORLIK

Of course, I understand the gentleman last night
was your boss, and the old one was your father
and I daresay this one's your husband.

BOBBY

No. Oh, no.

MRS. GORLIK

[*Icily*] Then the door stays open.

BOBBY

Very well.

MRS. GORLIK

It's ten o'clock and I suppose you know there's no gentlemen callers allowed after ten.

BOBBY

Mr. O'Neil was just going.

MRS. GORLIK

Yes, the gentlemen are always just going! — It's ten o'clock!   [*She goes.*]

BOBBY

I guess you'll have to go, Rims.

RIMS

[*Taking his hat*] All right.

BOBBY

Goodnight, dear.

RIMS

So we're not married any more?

BOBBY

No.

RIMS

That's nice.

BOBBY

It is, isn't it?

RIMS

When do I see you?

BOBBY

Whenever you like.

RIMS

And how do I see you? By appointment?

BOBBY

I'm not very busy — if we never had been married and I was just a girl you wanted to see sometime — how would you manage it?

RIMS

I could call you up tomorrow and take you for a bus-ride, I suppose. And dinner at Child's. Wouldn't that be grand?

BOBBY

I'd like it. Why don't you?

RIMS

Well, I don't want to go bus-riding — Aw Bobby, what's it all leading up to anyway. Are we going to get a divorce?

BOBBY

If you like.

RIMS

Will you marry me again if we do?

BOBBY

Oh, Rims, you are a darling! You are! Would you really do it all over again?

RIMS

Sure I would.

BOBBY

But you never really wanted to get married, did you? Now tell the truth —

RIMS

I wanted you.

BOBBY

Of course you did, but you didn't want a house. I wanted you but I didn't want a house. And I don't now.

RIMS

How do I know you won't fall for somebody else sometime? If I leave you here?

BOBBY

You don't.

RIMS

Oh.

BOBBY

How do I know you won't fall for somebody else? I don't. I don't want to. You aren't to

see me unless you just can't keep away. You
used to know me so well you didn't like me. You
used to know where I was and what I was doing
all the time. It was positively indecent, and we
won't have any more of it. It's like not wearing
any clothes.

RIMS

Well. All right.

BOBBY

So — now we're really free.

RIMS

I said all right. I don't give a whoop about that.

BOBBY

What do you give a whoop about?

RIMS

[*Close to her*] About you, you little fool! Can't
you see it? Don't you see I can't get along without you? I can't stand being away from you all
the time. I keep waking up in the night wanting
you.

BOBBY

So do I.

RIMS

I want to see you to-night.

BOBBY

Well — ?

RIMS

And the house is standing there waiting for us.

BOBBY

[*Turning away*] It'll just have to wait, then.
I got you into it in the first place — and you
didn't like it — and I didn't like it. And now,
thank God, we're out of it.

RIMS

I don't know what you want.

BOBBY

I don't either. I only know what I don't want.

RIMS

All right! [*He puts on his hat and goes out.*]

BOBBY

Goodbye. [*There's no answer. She stands still
for a moment, then closes the door and sits dis-
consolately on the edge of the bed. There is a
knock and she turns to the door. It's only* MRS.
GORLIK.

MRS. GORLIK

Have all the gentlemen gone?

BOBBY

Yes, Mrs. Gorlik. I'm sorry — but all the gentlemen have gone.

MRS. GORLIK

[*Looking behind the door*] I'm just seeing for myself. Don't you try any tricks. I try to run —

BOBBY

[*Over her shoulder, annoyed*] I know — a respectable house.

MRS. GORLIK

Don't try any tricks. [*She goes out, closing the door.* BOBBY *sits for a moment, disconsolate, then gets her night things from the closet and climbs on a chair to turn out the wall-lamp. She starts to undress, then falls on the bed, sobbing.* RIMS *appears outside the window in the moonlight. He opens the window, climbs in softly, and tiptoes to the package containing the bolt. As he places the bolt against the door in the semidark he startles* BOBBY *with the metallic click.*]

BOBBY

[*Looking up*] Oh, Rims!

RIMS

> [*Pointing to the screw driver on chair*] Bring me the screw driver, will you, dear?

BOBBY

> [*Bringing it to him*] Hush!   [RIMS *starts to fit the bolt to the door.*]

CURTAIN